PREGNANT IN THE SPIRIT

How to birth a life of TOTAL fulfillment-
Your True Purpose

PRINCESS-O'DILIA

PUBLISHED BY
2B-REAL PUBLISHING, LLC

© 2009 Princess-O'dilia

Pregnant in the Spirit

First Edition 2009
ISBN 0-9763312-1-7
ISBN 978-0-9763312-1-6

Written by Princess-O'dilia

Published by:
2B~Real Publishing, LLC
1000 South Old Woodward
Suite 105-2
Birmingham, MI 48009-6729
www.brealpublishing.com
pis08@brealpublishing.com
www.princessodilia.blogspot.com
www.blogtalkradio.com/quietnomore
www.christmovement.org
Phone: (888) 982-4377
Fax: (888) 609-2224

Thanks to all of my family. I love you all!

Thanks to my God Mother, Doris Williams. Thanks for your nurturing and unconditional love you've given me and the children. Thank you for your support and believing in this mission. Thanks for the core woman values that you also taught me along with my Mom. I love you for everything!

Thanks Dr. Richard L. Blanding (Granddaddy-Dad), Grandma Curvie Jones-Blanding, Aunt Glena, Uncle Sunny, Aunt Barb and Uncle Bill, Shelly, Jeff and Dr. Charles A. Fuget (Grandpa Chuck). Thanks to our Aunt Henrietta Henderson-Childs (Auntie) and family, Aunt Dianne, Aunt Ann, Aunt Gwen (we miss you!) and Uncle Greg and family, and Aunt Regina. Thanks for believing, understanding, and never wavering in your unconditional love! Your love can not be more appreciated! It's an example of God's love! We love you for doing what you didn't have to do.

In loving memory of Grandma (Mom), Dr. Audrea Fuget, we know that you are where we'll one day be. Your life was an inspiration and we'll eternally be grateful to all of your love, support, wisdom, knowledge, and guidance that you gave to us when you were here and will forever be long lasting in our minds as we live our lives. We love you and miss you!

I have the deepest gratitude to the entire staff at New Life Book Distributors! A special thanks to Richard, Sabrina and Brian for everything! I will forever be grateful and may God richly bless you and your business!

Additional thanks to my proofreaders (Aunt Linda, Melvin Patton, Gabrielle Lawson, and Tom B.) Thank you for your help!

Dedication

I dedicate this book in memory of my Grandmother, Audrey E. (McClain) Horne, aka "Mother". When growing up and as a young adult, Mother never judged me, but loved me. It is for her support and words of wisdom that she offered through the course of life that I will forever cherish and be eternally grateful. It is for her unselfish giving and strength that helped me keep my head up through some very rough times in my life. When I felt that I could go to no other Christian, I could always turn to Mother who would give me no judgment, but love, at the same time speaking truth that may even sometimes hurt.

I love and miss you Mother!

PREGNANT IN THE SPIRIT

How to birth a life of TOTAL fulfillment-

Your True Purpose

BY
PRINCESS-O'DILIA

Table of Contents

INTRODUCTION

What Is Spiritual Pregnancy?

Spiritual Pregnancy is the process of attaining True Purpose in your life. This intangible process (conception to manifestation) is accomplished only with one's choice of being guided by God's Spirit that is within and one's willingness to be free from the bondages of religion and the traditional processes of man. Hence, one lives an eternal life of fulfillment, peace, freedom without condemnation, gaining control of one's life's obstacles, obtaining an infinite measure of knowledge, wisdom and understanding that can not otherwise be obtained.

***

Spiritual pregnancy is very parallel to natural pregnancy with regards to the terms used to define its process (e.g., conception, delivery, postpartum depression, abortion, labor, etc.), with the exception of a few terms for example, period vs. trimester. Although very similar in terms, it is not similar in its tangible nature neither its gender prejudice. For example, in the spirit realm we are all capable of spiritual pregnancy.

From the beginning God gave us free will. Free will to accept Jesus Christ as our personal Lord and Savior; free will to obey; free will to love or hate; free will to do whatever we've chosen to do in our lives, etc. Nonetheless, there is coming a time when we near the end of another era in life. In this era, either you'll follow the plan that was predestined for you or nothing else will work.

Unfortunately, many of you may be a bit hard-headed, which may cause things to get a bit rough in your life. Many will find yourselves transitioning even at a point you thought you were comfortable or even stable. In this era, God is going to shake the earth! Can you say, "Hello, Holy Spirit?!"

As a people we have advanced on many different levels: technology, education, medicine and in so many other areas. Although spirit realm is no different, the interpretation of advancement is in reference to the degree of revelation. God didn't just give us the revelation of His Word all at once; He planned for the maturity of the times (Ephesians 1:10). In His mercy, He has met us where we've been. For example, with regards to the profound revelation of "Purpose" today or the message of "Prosperity" just a few years ago, if discussed even just 50 years ago would not have been considered an option for many reasons (man, technology, education, level of confidence, etc.).

I love God because He is strategic in His thinking and His distribution of knowledge and wisdom upon the earth. At this point, we've explored the earth and the moon. Through the benefit of education and research, a man can do and be most anything in most parts of the earth, which is great. We have great confidence in what "we" are able to do with the right resources at our finger tips. Consequently, this has also brought us to a point where many can derive the concept: my ability, my intellect, my opportunity, my, my, my, my.

Unfortunately, once you've mastered the "MY" concept, you can lose site of *True Purpose*-God's Desires for your life outside of salvation as a first thought for your life's dreams, goals, and aspirations. Are any of these phrases familiar to you? "Lord, I", "So, will you," or, "I" and then, "Lord, make it happen because this is what I want"? This concept of "my" opens the window for other belief factors outside of the realm of God. You become so focused on your own ability, you can lose site of God's ability and plan for your life, which is the ultimate fulfillment.

We are taught in John 14:26 that **"The Holy Spirit will teach us all things!"** To consider God's complete ability aside salvation is a phenomenon as it relates to one's dreams, goals, and aspirations. Most commonly, we direct our entire focus on man's process for our lives: go to school, get the degree, and become "successful". Or, we base our accomplishments on the level of degree we've received here on this earth. Jesus said in Matthew 16:26: *For what will it profit a man if he gains the whole world and forfeits his life [his blessed life in the kingdom of God]? Or what would a man give as an exchange for his [blessed] life [in the kingdom of God]?* Nevertheless, God let's us know in Ephesians 1:11 that He already had a perfect plan predestined for us.

In Him we also were made [God's] heritage (portion) and we obtained an inheritance; for we had been foreordained (chosen and appointed beforehand) in accordance with His purpose, Who works out everything in agreement with the counsel and design of His [own] will..."

God desires for us all to be positioned right on the earth so that we can live a Totally Fulfilled life! Everything that we've done has all been a part of the plan. Now that we have the confidence and boldness to be who we want to be in this life by the provisions that man has afforded us (all made possible through God), He wants us to completely turn our pilots on to *True Purpose* - God's plan for our lives which you now hold the keys through <u>Pregnant in the Spirit</u>.

Be a witness for God just as Jesus was! Now that you've experienced man's plan, learn what it's like to be completely guided by the Holy Spirit, without the bondages of man or religion. With regards to religion, learn to see God outside of the realm of the religious doctrine that you may participate. Establish a personal relationship with God so that He can *freely* work through you the impossible, the out-the-box, the radical, unexplained miracle through you. God wants you to accept and share His freedom, His love, His Joy, His Power and His Ability without the bondage of any man! God desires for you to live a life of fulfillment so that others may see God's goodness through you and may come to know God too!

CHAPTER 1

A Personal Note From The Author

Regardless of where you are, what you've done, what you've become, what you've accomplished or what mistakes you've made, your life has ONLY JUST BEGUN!

A Personal Note From The Author

A must read…

Nearly 4 months after the initial submission of Pregnant in the Spirit and some unforseen issues with editing, the Holy Spirit led me to continue writing. Each day was a day that I wanted this book to be done so that I could submit the final copy. However, through the inspiration of the Holy Spirit I continued to write. I now sit on the floor with my work around me, in awe of what has just transpired in my life, at the same time, feeling slightly in a *trance* and a little nervous as a result of the revelation and the demand that I feel is being placed on my life as a result of this experience. "Lord, please don't let me fail this assignment that you've given me. Continue to give me wisdom and knowledge." I pray to myself.

Prior to writing this book I thought I knew God, but by the end of the book I realized that I had only begun to know God. What I was inspired to write at times was so contrary to my then beliefs as a result of the religious bondage in my mind. It has taken years for me to begin to accept my freedom. Even now I must admit, "If I would have known the message of this book in its entirety, I can't say that I would have had the courage to write <u>Pregnant In the Spirit</u>"

Initially, I thought there was one message to be derived from <u>Pregnant in the Spirit</u> which was the process of attaining *True Purpose*. Thereby, one yielding the opportunity of peace, joy, confidence, and fulfillment through this process described as spiritual pregnancy. How wonderful! I was truly excited to share this revelation that would definitely cause more people to experience a fulfilled, peaceful, and joyful life as a result of the experience of spiritual pregnancy. I was also excited for the mission of enlightening the world of how the parallel between natural and spiritual pregnancy brings a great understanding and confidence to endure an intangible, blind, and scary, yet fulfilling process required to attain *True Purpose* in one's life. All of this accomplished through wisdom, knowledge and understanding inspired by the complete guidance of the Holy Spirit; thereby, offering the key to life's peace, confidence and fulfillment that all of mankind seek, yet today remains a phenomenon. However, God had an even greater plan. The Holy Spirit said, "They must *first* be free to operate with me in this era – to accomplish this process."

If then you have died with Christ to material ways of looking at things and have escaped from the world's crude and elemental notions and teachings of externalism, why do you live as if you still belong to the world? [Why do you submit to rules and regulations?—such as] (Colossians 2:20).

Once you accept the opportunity to be completely guided by the Holy Spirit (Romans 8:4-5, 9; Galatians 5:16), then and only then will you attain *True Purpose*. Have you ever heard the saying, "You ain't seen nothin' yet."? Well, if you believe that you've found your dream, but did not attain your dream under the guidance of the Holy Spirit, I dare you to follow this process of spiritual pregnancy, which yields you the perfect plan, the ultimate outcome, and the most fulfilling life you could ever imagine. Through this process you will receive complete satisfaction in every area of your life as you strive to attain the *True Purpose* that was designated for you! How can I say that? It is God's plan, a perfect work attained by His power through you! A process that you must initiate and allow Him to do through you.

To be guided by the Holy Spirit is to allow the Holy Spirit to guide you; teach you all things; intercede for you; do the impossible through you; and to be your friend and confidant (John 14:26). However, you must have the wisdom, knowledge, and understanding of how to properly discern what is God and what is not, while under this control of the Holy Spirit. You must also have understanding and awareness of the opposition and how to attain the victory regardless of what obstacles you may face in your life. You should have a thorough understanding of the process, described in <u>Pregnant in the Spirit</u> as *spiritual pregnancy* from the point of conception to the manifestation of the gift that God will birth through you (the impossible, the unbelievable thing).

To lack understanding of this intangible process, usually results in a spiritual abortion for many (to avoid or kill God's plan for your life). Just as in a natural pregnancy, spiritual pregnancy has some periods that will bring some discomfort and/or pain to your flesh. However, due to its intangible nature and until now nothing to definitively reference, many have been spiritually aborting the spiritual pregnancy process in their life. To prevent the catastrophic occurrence of spiritual abortion in your life, you must have the wisdom and knowledge necessary to make it through the process.

Honestly, as strong as my desire is to operate in complete control of the Holy Spirit and please God through that fulfillment, again, I can't say that I would have had the courage to write this book if I would have known the message in its entirety from the beginning. Some reading this book may be completely bound by man's traditional life's cycle and expectations and others may be bound by religion or both. It wasn't until I began to write this book that I realized how bound I had been as a result of religious bondages. I'm required to come back to God and yet know Him further. As a result, I am surprised of the even deeper truth behind His love, His freedom, His concepts, His views of religion, His views of man's plans and processes and the rank they have in our lives, His views of "sin", His views of fulfillment, His views of condemnation and judgment, His mere perception of man and the profound revelation of the spirit realm and how it relates to our lives.

Once God began to reveal to me the intent of the book, I had initially determined that the religious, the "church people" were not going to be ready for such a message. Although I wanted the world to receive this profound revelation, I had accepted that from where I came, the religious bondages would hold many back. God wants all to hear and understand because now is the time for change. Therefore, God proceeded to establish a solid foundation of understanding as it relates to real life so that this message may be understood and received by the world. God has taken spirit realm operation, interpreted by many as metaphysics or for others considered a perceived notion in such a way that all can hear, gain understanding and relate this intangible process to one's life.

Through the spiritual birth of <u>Pregnant in the Spirit</u>, it was revealed to me by the Holy Spirit that God lacks interest in "religion", due to His strong desire for a personal relationship with you, without the influences of man's concepts, restrictions, condemnation, judgments or bondages. What this means is that more importantly to God is your relationship with Him, not that with man, nor its entities. God is not interested in the religious identity and its guidelines, traditions, and regulations. This is not to say that those that are religious are bad or not children of God. Nevertheless, I am saying that God's children are God's children regardless and a religion doesn't define that. Once the religious concept is established in the mind, it is difficult to see outside of that box; thereby, preventing many from really seeing who "God" is without seeing "God" through the concepts of the religion. Thereby, you lack the ability to see all of God's creation as it relates to their position through the eyes of God, without judgment or condemnation, but with love. Without love, which is who God is, you lack the ability of attaining the *True Purpose* God designed for you.

As I have experienced the birthing of <u>Pregnant in the Spirit</u>, the position of the religious, the educated, the accomplished, and the scientists, I've often pondered in my mind. I've thought, "Although all long for the results of this intangible process, how will people freely accept this revelation?" Needless to say, regardless of what I've pondered in my mind during this process, God's profound message of spiritual equality, love, power, peace, confidence, wisdom, knowledge, and understanding of all things, freedom and complete fulfillment attained through the power of the Holy Spirit is loud and clear. Bottom-line, this is a spiritual awakening and it is the answer to the prayers of us all and God will speak to the hearts of man regarding this revelation.

Until I was free, I had no clue I was bound...

About 2 years ago, God sent two different people to tell me that God wanted me to Himself. God also sent one of them to tell me that I didn't know God and that I was determining my knowledge of God based on my past experiences. I had no idea what God would show me but I asked God, "Show me you if I don't know you." Shortly after that request, as I was driving down the highway one morning, I got a vision of God that made me laugh. God said, "I'm a little bit of this, and I'm a little bit of that". So the journey began...

A deeper freedom and confirmation...

As a result of the changes in <u>Pregnant in the Spirit</u>, the Holy Spirit led me to rewrite the Introduction once I had completed the book. I was away from home and as I set in my friend's room praying for the words for my personal note to you, I looked to the left and pulled a book off of a book shelf. Not to read but to glance at its Bibliography as a tutorial.

Not noticing what book I picked up (<u>Conversation with God</u> – an uncommon dialogue by Neale Donald Walsch), I took the book back where I was sitting and began to search for the Bibliography. My friend is a Unitarian, so the last thing I would expect is a book about God based on my then perception of all Unitarians. I was curious to know what my friend had found so important to bookmark so I began to read the page. At first I was completely offended as I immediately judged the sentence read, which was sexual. To my surprise, the Holy Spirit admonished me to read further, which at first seemed a little strange to me. Well, I couldn't stop reading about these conversations this Author was having with God. Ironically, some of the same conversations that God had with Mr. Walsch in 1993, God had recently with me in 2008, but *I* was merely frightened of the message God had given me. "God is that really who you are? Wow! I had no clue!" I would think often times.

Just previous that moment, I had been battling with the revelation that God had given me concerning some writing in Pregnant in the Spirit. "If this is the message that you've given "me" then the readers will get the same message when they read my book." I could just imagine God thinking aloud, *"Duh...what did you think?"* Well, I did not want to be "responsible" for this message! Many times throughout this process I've felt like Jesus did in the garden of Gethsemane (Matthew 14:36). Lord, "take away this cup from me".

Although, there were things in his book which I would personally seek further guidance (I did not read the book in its entirety), much of the conversation that I did read was parallel to the revelation that I had recently been given by the Holy Spirit. Although we may have used different ways to express the same thing a few times, the bottom-line was that God talked to us both in a way that we could understand. Therefore, I won't squabble over words, the metaphors, or phrases that mean the same thing, but said differently. For example, I often use the phrase, "guided by the 'Holy Spirit' which is the guidance of God's Spirit within you and he may use the phrase, "guided by my 'God Consciousness'".

One common and unfortunate summary of the dialogue with God that both Mr. Walsch and I had is that there is a misinterpretation of who God really is. Consequently, many people have not experienced the true freedom and love in God due to this misinterpretation. Consequently, many people that are experiencing God don't acknowledge it and there are many people who feel they know God but don't know Him at all. God's children are divided and many people don't confess Jesus Christ (The act of accepting the work of God through the life of Jesus Christ when He walked the earth and expressing the willingness to continue the same mission and purpose that He did of sharing the love and freedom of God, without judgment and condemnation for all of mankind. Thereby, being a follower of Christ [accepting Christ as your personal Lord and Savior]).

The distortion is that God is a God of condemnation and there are these rules and regulations that one must at all times maintain in order to be in right relationship with God. In fact, it is quite the contrary to the true and living God, one of love, freedom and no condemnation to man! Many people that have experienced God in the profound spiritual expression of love, freedom and joy, often times will not associate the experience they've encountered as the power of God within them. So even they lack the ability of rising to another spiritual level in God and attaining a life of fulfillment without even knowing.

In my teachings, I give a parallel to Jesus' walk and the walk of the late Dr. Martin Luther King who most people openly honor his life's purpose today by continuing to live the dream of freedom for all, in love and with no judgment or condemnation. Wouldn't it be great if we could all enjoy God together, honor Jesus' life's purpose today, along with a life of eternal freedom, confidence, joy, peace, and fulfillment through the power of God within us, without judgment and condemnation for one another?

Hmmm... Freedom - a very strong word...

In Conversation with God, the Author dictates his communication with God in the book. Some of his dictation that came from his conversation with God coincides with the message that God has given me regarding the requirement for this era in order to attain your *True Purpose*, God's plan for you, including my once position, "I already know God."

> *"Yet I invite you to a new form of communication with God. A two-way communication. In truth, it is you who have invited Me."*

As God has shown me as well as other people, I'm sure God doesn't just speak in an audible voice. God also speaks through strong feeling, experience, the Word of God, other reading materials, etc. The issue for many is not if God is speaking to you; however, it is discerning and then acting on what God is leading you to do. Mr. Walsch quotes God to say:

> *"...some people are willing to actually listen. They are willing to hear, and they are willing to remain open to communication even when it seems scary, or crazy, or downright wrong."*

I once thought, "There is a way that seems right unto a man, but the end there of is destruction, as many use the phrase, was referring to my questioning some guidelines and restrictions within religion

(Galatians 6:8; Romans 8:13; Proverbs 10:29; Matthew 7:13). I later realized that God was referring to you following your own way as opposed to the way that He has already planned. God's plan sometimes may seem wrong or may simply make no common sense because you've been use to your own way. I often refer to I Corinthians 2:14 where we're informed that without the wisdom and knowledge of God the spirit realm will seem foolish and unwise. Thereby, we are to trust God and not lean on our own understanding (Proverbs 3:5).

I once wrote a poem, *Jehovah, Your Provider,* and I'll quote, "If it is too hard for you, you're more than likely on the right track. How else can God get all of the Glory!" Again, don't put God in a box because God operates completely outside the box – far from your wildest imagination. God will reveal mysteries to you and these mysteries will cause you to awe at what God has accomplished through you! Mr. Walsch quotes God to say:

> *"Go ahead and act on all that you know. But notice that you've all been doing that since time began. And look at what shape the world is in. Clearly, you've missed something. Obviously, there is something you don't understand. That which you do understand must seem right to you, because 'right' is a term you use to designate something with which you agree. What you've missed will, therefore, appear at first to be 'wrong'. The only way to move forward on this is to ask yourself, "What would happen if everything I thought was 'wrong' was actually 'right'?"*

I say trust God! God's Power, God's Authority, God's Joy, God's Truth and you take one step forward to experiencing a profound change in your life!

I want to take one more quote from this book, <u>Conversation with God</u> as Mr. Walsch quotes God:

"You cannot know God until you've stopped telling yourself that you already know God. You cannot hear God until you stop thinking that you've already heard God. I cannot tell you My Truth until you stop telling Me yours."

At the end of the day, do you believe in God? Do you believe in the purpose of Jesus Christ and the power of the crucifixion? To allow God to share who He really is would eliminate many religious bondages often practiced within the church and would relinquish the concept that man's way is the only way for a life of fulfillment. Thereby, introducing to our world a new era, a new concept, a new way of life and approach to eternal freedom, confidence, peace, joy and fulfillment within our lives!

After this experience, I can truly say that I know God better now than I've ever known God before and I will continue to get to know God! What am I now? I confess no religion, I am a child of God, I am a follower of Jesus Christ, and I am completely guided by the Holy Spirit. That would be me. Now, will you take the opportunity to experience this journey?

Requirements for Spiritual Pregnancy

- Accept "No Condemnation"
- Allow the Holy Spirit (The Spirit of God) to Guide You!

Also see Chapter 5 for Spiritual Maternity Clothes
(The Armor of God)

Requirements for Spiritual Pregnancy

Many of you may be challenged with merely grasping the concept that God's Plan for you may be completely different from the plan you have mapped out for yourself. Aside many having to accept the reality that God's plan may be different than yours, I believe that a greater majority may be challenged with accepting that you don't have to be at some particular level in God for you to begin the process of spiritual pregnancy or to be worthy of living this life of fulfillment attained through Spiritual guidance. As this Spiritual process begins, God will work with each of His children as He wills.

For years many have been bound by religious traditions, man-made conditions and some very wrong ideologies regarding the true meaning of righteousness. This misconception or should I say, the lack of revelation of the true meaning of righteousness and who God really is has hindered many from a life of fulfillment. Leaders placing degrees on sin, judgment taking place amongst the children of God and even other people in the world being judged by the children of God, and I could go on, but I won't; you'll read about love in Chapters 5 and 6. Consequently, people have avoided God and denounced the call of God on their life.

I believe there has been so much judgment and condemnation derived from those professing to be "children of God" until God has been blamed for the attributes of man. Furthermore, the religious traditions and man-made conditions that are established in many religious practices are completely contrary to how God operates and is not indicative of His character. God is a God of love (John 3:16)! Who are we to judge anyone? The bible says in Luke 6:37:

*Judge **not**, and ye shall **not** be judged: condemn **not**, and ye shall **not** be **condemned**: forgive, and ye shall be forgiven.*

If you acknowledge the Word of God as it truly is, you will realize that you are NOTHING without God! You would realize that your righteousness has nothing to do with "your" works. God already took care of what would have been considered a reason for condemnation for us all through the crucifixion of our Lord and Savior Jesus Christ (II Corinthians 5:21: *For He hath **made Him to be sin for us**, who knew no sin; that **we might be the righteousness of God in Him**).*   Your righteousness is through Jesus Christ and you are not condemned! Read Romans 3:22-27:

*Even the righteousness of God which is by faith in Jesus Christ unto all and upon all them that believe: **for there is no difference**. For all have sinned and come short of the glory of God; Being justified freely by his grace through the redemption that is in Christ Jesus: Whom God hath set forth to be a propitiation through faith in his blood, to declare his righteousness for remission of sins that are past, through the forbearance of God; To declare, I say, at this time his righteousness: that he might be just, and the justifier of him which believeth in Jesus. Where is boasting then? It is excluded. By what law? Of works? Nay: but by the law of faith.*

That is so…Powerful! In verse 22: *"unto all and upon all*

them that believe: for there is no difference". So, regardless of your religion, if you've volunteered in the church 100 times, you're no different than the person that served 10 times in the church. If you believe in God and believe that through the sacrifice of Jesus Christ you were made righteous but you were hanging out last night with friends and got drunk, you slept with 5 men this week or 5 women this week, in God's eyes you're no less righteous than the person that believes and went to church 20 times this week, never had a drink, never fornicated in their life? Why? In the Word of God it is written that through the redemption that is in Christ Jesus, you are justified freely by His grace (Romans 3:24). According to the Word of God, the children of God are no different. We are all a work in progress. We have all sinned and have come short of the glory of God (Romans 3:23).

What's embarrassing for me is that I've heard these scriptures all of my life; however, it wasn't until I started writing my first book, The Armor of God that I received a portion of the revelation of Righteousness from the Holy Spirit. Immediately, I knew that the religious would struggle with this revelation as a majority. This revelation as it really is means once you're saved you're always saved regardless of whatever you do, say, or choose to be. Don't throw the book. It is what it is. However, when you answer the call of God on your life, it causes you to be separate, consecrated and holy before the Lord. Through the guidance of the Holy Spirit, who will teach you all things including God's commands for you as a child of God, you will learn how to walk in love, without judgment and you will become more dependant on the Holy Spirit for your guidance than your own selfish works, your religious traditions, or your man-made conditions. Who are you really? Nothing without God! Nothing!

No Condemnation!

Some of you believe that in order for you to move into the direction that God is calling for you that you've got some Religious standard that you must meet. Or, you may even feel that you must give up every bad habit in your life. Quite the contrary! Again, as you take the step towards *True Purpose* in your life you will become more like God. He's not asking you to do anything but make that step towards fulfillment. God knew that you were not without sin from the beginning, which was the purpose for the sacrifice of Jesus Christ. Wow! Jesus started the Movement for Spiritual Equality. What a Movement! According to John 3:18, *"He that believeth on Him is **not condemned**: but he that believeth **not** is **condemned** already, because he hath **not** believed in the name of the only begotten Son of God."*

> From the beginning, God had a plan for you. He knew everything that you would do, what you would say, how you would walk...

Let's refer back to the American Heritage College Dictionary, condemned: "1. To express strong disapproval of. 2. To pronounce judgment against; sentence. 3. To judge or declare to be unfit for use or consumption." Did you just read one of the definitions of condemned as: "to judge or declare to be unfit for use or consumption"? Well, the Bible says that you are NOT CONDEMNED, which means that you are "not" to be judged and you are "not" unfit for use or consumption if you believe in the only begotten Son of God. However, if you do not believe in the only begotten Son of God, you are already condemned.

What does that mean for the one that doesn't believe in Jesus Christ or the one that believes in the life of Jesus Christ, but doesn't believe that He was the Son of God, born of the Spirit and flesh as indicated in the Holy Bible? What about the one that believes that Jesus was a leader and prophet, but doesn't believe that Jesus was born with a purpose to die for all of mankind, let alone so that *all* could have a direct relationship with God? Finally, the one that doesn't believe in anything the Holy Bible has to say as TRUTH? For whom one or more of these scenario questions may apply, before you read any further, I invite you to read Chapter 8 of this book now. (Not to convince you, but to invite you to a new concept or philosophy on Jesus).

My philosophy: To not have the revelation of the LOVE, POWER, FREEDOM, and PEACE demonstrated through the life and death of Jesus as a spiritual being is to not be capable of believing the impossible God wishes to do through you. As you've read in Chapter 8, God wants no division between us and Jesus is a child of God just like you are. As you read in "The Personal Note from the Author", I choose to consider God as my Father as many do. Although some choose to not identify God as a he or a she and that's fine, that's all relevant to the Truth that God is the Father (the Head) of Truth, Love, Power, Eternal Freedom, Peace and Joy. God the Father (the Head) is the key to the seemingly impossible becoming a reality for your life!

Summary: to believe in the only begotten Son of God, Jesus Christ, you honor God by your belief of the impossible and you show love, honor and respect for the sacrifice that was made for us from God and through the life and death of the leader in our mission to God, Jesus. So, regardless of where you are in your walk with God, you qualify for spiritual pregnancy. God will meet you wherever you are, but to birth a life of TOTAL fulfillment, you must "Believe" what seems to be the impossible! OK, let's continue...

From the beginning, God had a plan for you. He knew everything that you would do, what you would say, how you would walk, and so on and on. You are God's handiwork and He has already predestined the good works for you (Ephesians 2:10). We don't have to be perfect as we read in the scripture and in the example of Mary in Chapter 3. As she was blessed with favor and she was to conceive our Lord and Savior Jesus Christ after the Holy Spirit would come upon her, so shall it be for us (Luke 1:28, 35). God lets us know in His word that He has no respect of persons (II Chronicles 19:7). Therefore, what He will do for one of His children He will do for another one of His children.

Allow the Holy Spirit (The Spirit of God) to Guide You!

"In [this] freedom Christ has made us free [and completely liberated us]; stand fast then, and do not be hampered and held ensnared and submit again to a yoke of slavery [which you have once put off]" (Galatians 5:1).

My favorite is Apostle Paul. He was very free in the Spirit and kept it real. *For you, brethren, were [indeed] called to freedom; only [do not let your] freedom be an incentive to your flesh and an opportunity or excuse [for selfishness], but through love you should serve one another* (Galatians 5:13). Yes, you are free, but to interpret what he was saying, "You're free in the Spirit, but don't get it confused that you can use this as an excuse for your flesh to run wild." Paul goes on a little further about what it means to be free in the Holy Spirit:

> *But I say, walk and live [habitually] in the [Holy] Spirit **[responsive to and controlled and guided by the Spirit]**; then you will certainly not gratify the cravings and desires of the flesh (of human nature without God). For the desires of the flesh are opposed to the [Holy] Spirit, and the [desires of the] Spirit are opposed to the flesh (godless human nature); for these are antagonistic to each other [continually withstanding and in conflict with each other], so that you are not free but are prevented from doing what you desire to do. But if you are guided (led) by the [Holy] Spirit, you are not subject to the Law* (Galatians 5:16-18).

Powerful! We are to be completely responsive to and guided and guided by the Holy Spirit! If we allow ourselves to be guided by the Holy Spirit and not "Man" – NO "Man" we don't have to worry about being controlled by our fleshly desires, because in Him we will possess the desires of the Spirit. Therefore, the requirement of spiritual pregnancy being predicated on you having a certain position in God is void of truth. You are not condemned; you are free; and you are to be completely responsive to and guided by the

Holy Spirit so that you may establish your right position in God here on this earth for the purpose of building the Kingdom of God!

CHAPTER 3

The Prime Examples

- Mary
- Elizabeth and Zechariah
- Jesus

The Prime Examples

> Mary's Spiritual Pregnancy was a prime example of how you will conceive in the Spirit...

Mary

In the beginning, God gave us the prime examples of what it is like to be pregnant in the Spirit. Our first example was Mary, a virgin handmaiden that found absolute favor with the Lord (Luke 1:30, 46). She was visited by the angel Gabriel to inform her that the Holy Spirit would come upon her and she would conceive a child (Luke 1:31). Mary's testimony of spiritual pregnancy is a great example of how powerful the Holy Spirit is and the possibilities that could take place in your life if you allow Him to reign.

In the passage about Mary's prophesy of her *True Purpose* given through the angel Gabriel (Luke 1:27-35), notice in verse 28, the angel Gabriel said to Mary, "...*O favored one (endued with grace)! The Lord is with you! Blessed (favored of God) are you before all other women!*" According to the American Heritage College dictionary, favor means: 1) **unmerited (not merited or deserved) divine assistance** given humans for their regeneration or sanctification; 2) a virtue coming from God... From the same dictionary, **sanctification** means 1) to set apart for sacred use, **consecrate.** 2) To make holy; purify.

Therefore, I believe that it is safe to say that although Mary was a virgin, this calling on her life to be the mother to Jesus Christ was not based on all of her "good" works. Nor was it based on her level of consecration or sanctification. OK Bible Scholars, I am not implying that she did not possess these attributes (consecration, sanctification, holiness).

Nonetheless, I am implying that it was not based solely on her attributes, good or bad. Yes, Mary was a virgin but it is not written that Mary was blameless of sin like it is written for example, about Zechariah and Elizabeth (Luke 1:6). Mary was not perfect; yet, she was highly favored before all women (Luke 1:28)!

Mary's Spiritual Pregnancy was a prime example of how you will conceive in the Spirit - the *favor* of God. There are some of you that may consider yourself to be like Elizabeth and Zechariah: righteous in the eyes of God and blameless in all the commandments of the Lord: consecrated, sanctified, and holy (Luke 1:6-7). Yet, you must keep in mind that as a result of the birth of Jesus Christ, those of you that believe are righteous through the sacrifice of Jesus Christ in the eyes of God (Philippians 1:11; Romans 5:21; 2 Peter 1:1). Praise God! It is not of your works, but the work of the crucifixion (2 Corinthians 5:21).

Just know this, for your obedience to the call on your life, you will find deliverance and total victory in your life. Not all the time will your life or walk with God be where you think it should be when answering to the call of God or being driven to the call of God. We're all a work in progress. Nevertheless, as a result of this spiritual birthing process you will gain a much closer relationship with God. Therefore, it's inevitable that via this process you will become more like God in every way. Now, let's get back to the story of Mary.

> Mary believed the impossible, the radical, the out-the-box, uncommon thing, and the non-common sense word from the Lord. Can you say, "I must believe the impossible?!" Let's continue…

Immediately after the angel Gabriel left Mary, she went to Elizabeth's house. I'm sure to confirm what the angel Gabriel said to her. You know how it is, even if we believe, we want to see some sort of reference or confirmation. Well, God had everything already planned out. The angel Gabriel had visited Zechariah, Elizabeth's husband about 6 months prior to his visitation to Mary and told him that he and his wife, both of very old age would bare a child (Luke 1:13-17, 26). However, Zechariah did not believe what the angel Gabriel prophesied to him (Luke 1:20). So, Zechariah began to call out the realities (common sense factors) that would seem likely to hinder this prophesy from happening (Luke 1:18). Well, God could not allow for Zechariah to speak against His promise; therefore, the angel Gabriel declared that Zechariah would be silent and be unable to speak until what God had promised was fulfilled and it came to pass just as the angel Gabriel said (Luke 1:20, 22). When Elizabeth became pregnant as the angel Gabriel prophesied, she secluded herself entirely for five months until Mary came to her, which was in the sixth month (Luke 1:24, 26). Therefore, no one knew of Elizabeth's pregnancy, but she and her husband Zechariah, whom God had silenced.

When Mary got to Elizabeth's house, the baby (John the Baptist) in Elizabeth's belly jumped and the Holy Spirit "took over" Elizabeth and Elizabeth began to prophecy to Mary as the Holy Spirit spoke through her (Luke 1:41). The Lord then confirmed through the prophecy of Elizabeth what the angel Gabriel had told Mary (Luke 1:42): *"And she cried out with a loud cry, and then exclaimed, Blessed (favored of God) above all other women are you! And blessed (favored of God) is the Fruit of your womb!"* The Holy Spirit later spoke through Elizabeth that it was because Mary **"believed"** what the Lord said to her that there would be fulfillment (Luke 1:45). Mary believed the impossible, the radical, the out-the-box, uncommon thing, and the non-common sense word from the Lord. Can you say, "I must believe the impossible?!" Let's continue...

After Mary received these words from the Lord, she began to worship and give God praise (Luke 1:46-55)! Can you imagine this? Mary was just informed that something would take place in her that could cost her relationship with her fiancé Joseph and let's not mention her life! In that time, for pre-marital sex, you were considered a whore and would be stoned to death for doing so. Who would believe such a thing could be true? Mary did. Mary "believed" the Word from the Lord and she PRAISED and WORSHIPED God before she experienced the conception from the Holy Spirit (the manifestation of the promise)! She trusted in the Lord to do whatever was necessary to bring His Purpose in her life to fulfillment. Let's read again what the Lord spoke through the angel Gabriel in Luke 1:37:

For with God nothing is ever impossible and no word from God shall be without power or impossible of fulfillment.

I want you also to recognize that becoming the Mother of Jesus Christ was only one part of Mary's call on her life by God. Mary was also called to be an example of holiness, endurance, submission, obedience, how to walk in love, and how to not hinder the call on our children's lives. When the angel Gabriel spoke to Mary, He did not tell her that her Son, Jesus Christ would be ridiculed and that He would be brutally beaten and crucified. He spoke of His beginning and His greatness, but he did not speak of His end. I'm sure Jesus spoke with His mother, just as He spoke to the disciples of His destiny, but, how do you think Mary responded when the revelation was told to her or confirmed to her what she probably had already felt in her Spirit and had been told by others? Possibly: "Lord, I don't remember this in the prophecy? "Lord, are you sure?" Could you imagine her thoughts or what she probably felt?

"Life and death are in the power of the tongue" (Proverbs 18:21).

Let's not forget, Mary was human just like you and I. She carried Jesus in her womb just like any other woman; which generally forms a bond between the mother and the child. Although, regardless of the pain or even anger I'm sure she felt as a mother, she had to remain humble and walk in love with all of Jesus' offenders just as Jesus did. Imagine for a moment, as Jesus continued to walk in love, His mother Mary acting irate, operating in strife, malice, and even hatred as a result of the attacks against her Son? I'm sure you could imagine many things you could have done if you would have been in her shoes. Let me just say, I don't know about you, but I know me. If someone would attack either of my children, I could see myself losing my cool and have done it before ("Lord, help me to be like Mary."). However, the reality for Mary was that she was a significant part of the purpose that Jesus had on His life and she had to stay the course just as Jesus did. What an example! Mary had to be an example, remain humble, walk in love, and keep the faith that what God spoke to her would be fulfilled at all cost; even if it cost her Son's life.

Elizabeth and Zechariah

Allow me to bring your attention to a few points regarding the story of Elizabeth and Zechariah. The Lord had also given a word to Zechariah of a gift that would be completely abnormal, radical, and uncommon as well, considering their situation of age and the fact that Elizabeth was barren (incapable of offspring) (Luke 1:12). However, Zechariah had unbelief in his heart (Luke 1:18). In order to prevent Zechariah from speaking contrary to the word of the Lord given through the angel Gabriel, God made Zechariah dumb until it came to pass (not just for the pregnancy, but also for the confirmation to Mary (Luke 1:20). How drastic and radical is that? As it is written, *"Life and death are in the power of the tongue"* (Proverbs 18:21). So, keep your mouth off of God's promises and people. If you don't understand something, just be quiet and wait on the Lord. Oftentimes what God calls you to do doesn't make common sense, not to mention the things that you will experience during the spiritual pregnancy. Don't worry and be obedient because God has it strategically mapped out.

What was required of Mary is required of us. We must believe the impossible; remain humble; walk in love; and keep the faith that what God says is so! We are to PRAISE and WORSHIP Him even before we receive the manifestation! What God has spoken for many of you to do, it is uncommon, out-the-box, radical, and seems to be humanly impossible to say the least. But, we know that with God ALL things are POSSIBLE if you just BELIEVE as Mary did (Luke 1:37; 45)! Furthermore, how better can God get ALL of the GLORY?!

God is the same yesterday, today and forever (Hebrews 13:8)! Just as He gave Mary unmerited favor, He has given you unmerited favor. Just as He gave confirmation to Mary, he will give you confirmation in your Spirit by the Holy Spirit. He may also give confirmation through people or even an angel (Hebrews 13:2). Jesus said in John 14:26:

> But the Comforter (Counselor, Helper, Intercessor, Advocate, Strengthener, Standby), the Holy Spirit, Whom the Father will send in My name [in My place, to represent Me and act on My behalf], He will teach you all things...

God wants you to be confident in Him. He doesn't want you to feel the need to depend or trust on someone having to inform you of your next move, or you feeling that you need someone to call you out in a revival to assure you that you're on the right track, etc. He needs you to know and trust the voice of the Holy Spirit!

You must also know that God's Word can always be backed up. If you seek confirmation, you will be able to find the confirmation because He's already set it up. For example, Elizabeth, who merely followed the guidance of the Holy Spirit with regards to her seclusion after she became pregnant, was God's divine order. I'm sure she was very excited to find that she

> **Mary was also frightened in the beginning, just like many of you may be.**

was pregnant and would have loved to tell at least a few people, but she hid herself (Luke 1:24). How perfect was this for the angel Gabriel to prophesy of something no one knew but God, Zechariah, and Elizabeth? Do you see how important it is for us to follow the guidance of the Holy Spirit?

Mary was also frightened in the beginning, just like many of you may be. Maybe an angel didn't walk in the room to announce a word to you, nor did a prophet call you out in a service to announce that this was going to happen, but in that small still voice, or maybe a word or direction, many of you know that God has called you for something that is uncommon, out-the-box, radical, and humanly impossible!

Again, you are to do as Mary did, say "YES" Lord to the call and Praise and Worship Him (the highest form of thanks), for with God NOTHING is impossible (Luke 1:37). You must also remember Proverbs 3:5 – King James Version:

> *Trust in the LORD with all thine heart; and lean not unto thine own understanding.*

Or, I love Proverbs 3:5 - Translation Version:

Lean on, trust in, and be confident in the Lord with all your heart and mind and do not rely on your own insight or understanding.

Jesus

As Jesus walked the earth feeling in the Spirit that He was the Savior of the world, and for that He would go through the most challenging and fulfilling spiritual pregnancy of all, it is interesting to think that Jesus was as you and I, man with purpose. Did Jesus realize that He had already seen glory and was just waiting for this earthly duty to be done so that He could go back to heaven to sit with His Father? Or as many believe, return back to Him? Was He able to recall Himself in Heaven, but now sitting amongst us with the understanding that He must just finish this purpose with the idea of going back where He came from? Or, was He completely reliant upon the Holy Spirit throughout His entire time here on earth with a knowing given to Him by the Holy Spirit that He was called and was the begotten son of God?

I strongly suggest that Jesus was not in Heaven before He was here but was created of God and is the only begotten son because He is the only child of God that was not born of a man and woman. I strongly suggest that Jesus knew in His Spirit that there was something special about Him and at a young age, as a result of the type of birth by which He came, knew that He was called for a great purpose. At a young age the Spirit of God began to reveal to Him the call on His life and that revelation of purpose was also given to His mother regarding His life before and after His birth (Luke 1:27-38). Jesus was created to be an example of how we should conduct our spiritual pregnancies. Through the Holy Spirit it was revealed to Him the call on His life. Through the Holy Spirit He was instructed where to go, what to do, and how to prepare for the different periods in His life (Acts 10:38).

I know many may say so confidently that Jesus was an exception to the rule. One may say, "He is Jesus for God's sake!" because of the life that He led, and that's the beauty of His existence. You must realize that Jesus was formed here in the "flesh" to be an example for you and to die so that you could have a life of fulfillment and have a personal relationship with God (I Peter 2:21). He was born with purpose just as you were. It's awesome to reflect on the life of Jesus and how He conducted the assignment of purpose in His life. Just as Jesus was led by the Holy Spirit, you are to be led by the Holy Spirit (e.g., Luke 2:27; 4:1). For example, Jesus gives honor to the Holy Spirit for the miracles that He performed (Matthew 12:28). Through His walk here on earth you can learn of love (John 3:16), how to react when faced with Seducing Spirits and the necessity to continuously abide in God (Matthew 4:1-11), how to handle the final stages of spiritual pregnancy (Matthew 26:36-46), how to handle betrayal (Matthew 26:47-53), and so... much more!

Jesus was able to stand and walk as He did only through the guidance of the Holy Spirit as He was here in the "FLESH".

According to Romans 8:3:

> For what the law could **not** do, in that it was weak through the flesh, God sending his own Son in the **likeness** of **sinful flesh**, and for sin, condemned sin in the flesh.

What an awesome revelation?! God wanted you and me to see that we can do it too, so He created Jesus as an example. For many of you your purpose may not seem as significant as dying for us heathens here on earth (OK, we aren't exactly heathens), but your purpose is significant for the salvation of many and God says that you can do it just as Jesus did.

For the spectators, this is not to minimize the significance of our Savior and Lord Jesus Christ. However, this is to provide you revelation given by the Holy Spirit that it is your requirement to do as God has planned for you and for you also to stand through all things as Jesus did. I don't believe that God ask of us anything that He didn't provide already as an example for us through the call of Jesus Christ (incl. the entire process from the conception of Mary to His resurrection). Jesus was our awesome example. He can honestly say, "I've been there, done that." I love it!

I was going to move on, but I wanted you to also notice that Jesus had a little character too. In His own way, He'd let you know of His position. Maybe, you won't read it like I read it, but consider this interpretation as Jesus gets a little sarcastic when the Pharisees question His authority to, in other words, "call it so". According to John 8:14, "Jesus answered, Even if I do testify on My own behalf, My testimony is true and reliable and valid, for I know where I came from and where I am going; but you do not know where I come from or where I am going." My interpretation: "You don't know me like that. Regardless if you believe me or not, it is what it is (there's nothing to prove), I know my authority in God – period! How many of you have been in a situation where you've had the revelation, but those around you thought you were either mentally unstable, thinking too far out-the-box, or had that "Who do you think you are" reaction towards you? Well, you are not alone; Jesus went through that as well.

Read what Jesus told Peter when he, out of "support" for Jesus, spoke against Jesus' Purpose.

From that time forth Jesus began [clearly] to show His disciples that He must go to Jerusalem and suffer many things at the hands of the elders and the high priests and scribes, and be killed, and on the third day be raised from death. Then Peter took Him aside to speak to Him privately and began to reprove and charge Him sharply, saying, God forbid, Lord! This must never happen to You!

But Jesus turned away from Peter and said to him, Get behind Me, Satan! ***You are in My way [an offense and a hindrance and a snare to Me]; for you are minding what partakes not of the nature and quality of God, but of men.*** (Matthew 16:21-23)

Do you recognize how adamant Jesus was? Don't ever forget, you are here on this earth to fulfill the Purpose that God has ordained for your life. It is God's will for you to live a life of fulfillment! You are here to build the Kingdom of God (bring more souls back to him) by answering the call of God on your life – living a life of fulfillment! Jesus said that if you desire to be His disciple to deny yourself (Matthew 16:24), which means to deny your way. As you read in this passage, you are partaking not of the nature and quality of God, but of men to not fulfill your *True Purpose*. He said to "follow me" and the Amplified translation reads further, "***conform wholly to My example in living and, if need be, in dying also***" (Matthew 16:24). God is so... AWESOME! He leaves nothing to the imagination!

Jesus' delivery period...

One of the most challenging periods in the pregnancy of Jesus, just as yours will be, is the period of delivery. It gets tougher the closer you get to the end of your pregnancy. Praise God! Through the experience of Jesus, you can feel confident that you're not alone, even when you are faced with feelings of depression and fear as you near the end of your delivery period, just to name a few front-line attacks from the enemy (Matthew 26:37-39). Jesus experienced that as well, just for you!

Through Jesus' experience, we also know that we must pray for our brothers and sisters that are experiencing spiritual pregnancy. We need each other as Jesus needed for Peter and the two sons of Zebedee to watch and pray with Him in Gethsemane just before the start of the crucifixion (Matthew 26:38, 40). So let's also adhere to the words He gave Peter and Zebedee in Matthew 26:41, "All of you must keep awake (give strict attention, be cautious and active) and watch and pray, that you may not come into temptation. The spirit indeed is willing, but the flesh is weak."

The enemy will aim attack on your confidence and faith; even causing you to doubt everything that you've believed during your pregnancy so that you will not go through with the delivery of *True Purpose* in your life! Although you may not be facing a treacherous death, you are facing the delivery of an eternal victory – one that will give Glory to God and get you placed in right position on the battlefield (the earth), which will ultimately result in the building of the Kingdom – A GREAT VICTORY; thereby yielding you a life of fulfillment! God just needs you to submit and trust Him 100% as

Jesus did in Matthew 26:39: *"...nevertheless, not what I will (not what I desire), but as You will and desire."*

"Stay the course like Jesus did! Just as I was with Jesus I am with you. No, you don't have to die for all of mankind, but in you I've also placed an awesome purpose that is just as significant for the battle to be won!" saith God!

CHAPTER 4

Key Hindrances of Spiritual Pregnancy
(e.g., barren)

- Cares of this World
- Fear, Doubt, and Unbelief

Key Hindrances of Spiritual Pregnancy
(e.g., Barren)

Cares of this World

For so long we've been conditioned by the world's system and the world's way of success. We get excited when someone accomplishes the dreams according to the world's standards, and that's OK However, would a person duplicate that same excitement if someone felt guided by the Holy Spirit to not follow man's process? If someone decided against College after High School, or decided to discontinue College because they felt "led" by the Holy Spirit to become "Supernaturally Certified"? I doubt it. In fact, I believe that eye brows would go up.

God is calling for a separate people who will not be conformed to this world, neither the processes of man. *"And be not **conformed** to this world: but be ye transformed by the renewing of your mind, that ye may prove what is that good, and acceptable, and perfect, will of God"* (Romans 12:2). Your decisions must come from God, His wisdom and His direction; which means, if God is calling for you to denounce college, or to change your career, or to close down your business, you must do whatever He requires of you. *"Roll your works upon the Lord [commit and trust them wholly to Him; He will cause your thoughts to become agreeable to His will, and] so shall your plans be established and succeed (Proverbs 16:3). "*

Consider the economy for a moment. Man's way isn't working

so well now is it? Absolutely not! To base your stability or happiness on a degree of any type, is not very wise these days. Currently, you could have a degree or 2 or 3 and lose everything in a moments notice. Or, your business to which you've devoted all of your time can plunge at anytime. What can you trust these days, except the Word of God, which He promises you that His word will not return unto Him void (Isaiah 55:11)? Chasing the processes of man, via a job or any career without God's divine order in this era, is pretty risky.

Let's admit; many of you are probably unfulfilled in your life, lacking TOTAL VICTORY. You're either tired, rushed, living from paycheck to paycheck, carrying the worries of this world on your shoulders, barely have time to prepare home cooked meals for your family, can barely find time to worship or spend time with God due to your "so" busy schedule, your kids are sent off to a baby sitter or a nanny for 40 hours a week, you barely have time to take a vacation, or, you don't even have the money to take a vacation, or your health is border-line fatal, etc. You may say, "That's OK, because I believe that God has healed me." Or, "I'm not confessing any of these things in my life." That is great! However, your TOTAL VICTORY will come as a result of your OBEDIENCE to the call of God on your life – you implementing *True Purpose* in your life (Deuteronomy 28:1-2; Job 12:13)! Without obedience, the challenges you continuously seem to face in your life (lack, disorder, etc.) will remain in your life as a revolving door, for there is no foundation to your purpose.

I know; some of you may feel that some challenges are just a part of "life". You may feel there is no way to get around some of these things. Well, I have news for you, "With God's Plan, you can"! God is a God of order and through His plan you'll find freedom, order, peace, joy, and time for God, you, and your family. God doesn't want another one of His children to leave this life unfulfilled (John 10:10; Psalm 91:16).

Imagine this…

"Betty sure did love the Lord. She stayed in that shack all of her life and barely had food to feed herself sometimes; but she stayed committed toward the call of the Lord. I'm glad she's gone on to be with the Lord. Now she can be peaceful and live eternally in heaven with her Father."

How sad! Unfortunately, this happens all the time. No, it is not all about money in any way; however, how much greater if she could have enjoyed life while she was here while fulfilling the call of God for her life?

The thief cometh not, but for to steal, and to kill, and to destroy: I am come that they might have life, and that they might have [it] more abundantly (John 10:10).

How many more lives could Betty have touched if she had the resources to go near and far for the call of God? Did Betty die with illness? Did she die of fatigue? Why exactly did Betty die? Could it had been the struggles that she faced in her life because she did not have the revelation that God called her to live a life of fulfillment? Did she not realize that she was a King's kid; that she was an heir of a Royal Priesthood (Romans 8:1; Galatians 3:16)?

We are in this world, but not of this world – literally (Romans 12:2)! How sweet it could have been if the comments after her death were:

"Betty sure did live an awesome life. She had so... much knowledge and wisdom and was so humble about everything. She gave to feed the hungry and would give her last if it came to that. I don't know what it was, but we never saw her working outside of ministry, but she always seemed to have the best, and never wanted for anything. She even left her children a great heritage and gave to other charities. God was really good to her and you could tell there was always something different about her. She loved God and others, and God 'truly' loved her."

How awesome would this be, when even from the outside looking in, all you can say for someone else's life is, "To God Be the Glory!"?

This is what God wants from His children: for all to live a fulfilled life and through that life, share His goodness. He wants us to trust Him as we trusted our parents when we were little children – innocent and not taunted by the ways of this world. Yes, for some, God will call to go to college and seek an education into XYZ field. However, it should be first acknowledged that maybe God didn't call you to go to college. Your *True Purpose* may or may not include college. God may just want to Supernaturally Certify you. Do you trust Him? Do you trust Him with your children and with you? Just a hint: Just because you didn't make it as you thought you should have to this point doesn't mean that it is due to the lack of a degree. Yes, many set backs have been due to the lack of money and credit awareness, but primarily as a result of not allowing God a chance to birth in you *True Purpose*.

Let's not waist time – let's become a *True Purpose* Driven People! Rather you make 1 Million, 1 Billion or simply a great debt free life and you've got enough to enjoy life, you've put a smile on God's face just by giving Him the opportunity to work through you fulfillment. We're not all called to make a Billion, but we're all called to attain *True Purpose*. We're all called to live a peaceful, joyful, and healthy life. We're all called to guide and bring others into the Kingdom of God and into the opportunity of eternal freedom, love and ultimately fulfillment for their life. We're all called to be missionaries and followers of the Movement that Jesus Christ led. We're all called to set an example for God! We're all called to take a stand for God! We're all called to serve God at all cost. Finally, we're all called to be separate from the world's system.

Fear, Doubt and Unbelief

What are you fearing, or having doubts about? Do you have doubt that God is going to do the impossible through you? Do you fear that you're going to look ridiculous to your family or friends? Do you doubt this spiritual process and its outcome? Are you already spiritually pregnant, but the road has gotten too rough, so you're contemplating a spiritual abortion? Whatever the scenario, just stand and keep the faith. Once you've delivered the gift that God has given you, there is a great reward at the end of the road. Whatever you do, don't give up and don't look back! You'll have plenty of time to reflect once you've made it through to the manifestation of the gift that is inside you.

Now, I do want to address the fear of financial despair. Based on current observation of this spiritual pregnancy process, many will experience financial hardship for a period of time and many will begin the process with a current situation of financial hardship. If you are afraid of how you're going to make it financially, do not be afraid any more! If God has instructed you to go into a specific direction, or if you believe you're headed in the "right" direction, but you're not sure, God knows your heart and your intent and He's "got your back"! Don't worry; regardless of how the situation looks, continue to trust God, thank Him for what He's already done and keep in mind, God is your provider! Don't get side tracked by your circumstance. When it seems as though you are overwhelmed, stop for moment and began to thank God!

Pray this prayer:

> *"God, I'm giving my financial situation up to you so that you can handle this for me. I can't do it, so right now I thank you for taking care of my situation. Lord, please change my heart in the direction that you want it to go so that I may do the right thing if you choose for me to do something in this matter. Thank you Father! Thank you for your faithfulness and the strength and faith that you've given me to release this completely over to you!"*

I'm inclined to believe that God is faithful based on my life! I'm also inclined to believe based on my observation of this spiritual pregnancy process, if you happen to fall on short times during this process that if you ride the wave and just hang in there, you will see the bright light at the end of the tunnel. If you have yielded to the plan God has for you, you will completely be satisfied and restored (Ephesians 2:10, Proverbs 16:3)! God wants you to completely understand and adapt to His Word which states in Philippians 4:19

that God will provide all of your needs according to His riches in glory. Unfortunately, due to the distraction of the circumstance, many are guilty of quoting the scripture, but not completely taking God at His Word. Again, God said that **He will** provide all of your needs according to **His riches in Glory**! So, are you afraid of financial stability? Or, is it, "What I feel He's calling me for, I'm not sure if I can do that?"

Regardless of your circumstance or reason for doubt, fear, or unbelief, you just need to know: "It is not your ability. It is God's ability!" You must yield to the Holy Spirit and trust Him (Proverbs 3:5). Jesus said in His Word that the Holy Spirit would teach you all things (John 14:26). What more do you need? I know, the "Scholars" of the world may say, "How can you encourage such a thing as to not consider college? God gives us "Common Sense"!" "We all have an opportunity to go to college, so we should all take that opportunity." "After all, God is the one that gave us these opportunities." Fair enough, that all makes "common sense". However, this is not "common sense", this is "revelation sense". As you read in Chapter 3, the miracles that took place within the lives of Mary and Elizabeth did not make "common sense"! God is the same yesterday, today, and forever (Hebrews 13:8)! He can and will do the same thing through you (e.g., uncommon, radical, out-the-box) only "if" you believe. **Warning**: Don't be like Zechariah as you read in Chapter 3 (Luke 1:20).

In this era, the Holy Spirit is going to overtake the earth with God's power! Things are going to happen within the earth in ways that man will not be able to explain. Unless you are operating in the Spirit, you will not be able to accept nor comprehend what the

Spirit of God is getting ready to do within the earth. He is getting ready to take us into a realm of "His Knowledge-His Revelation" that we've never experienced. "But the natural, non-spiritual man does not accept or welcome or admit into his heart the gifts and teachings and Revelation of the Spirit of God, for they are folly (meaningless nonsense) to him; and he is incapable of knowing them [of progressively recognizing, understanding, and becoming better acquainted with them] because they are spiritually discerned and estimated and appreciated" (I Corinthians 2:14). Can you say, "I want *True Purpose?*"

CHAPTER 5

Spiritual Maternity
Clothes & Accessories
THE FULL ARMOR OF GOD – (Ephesians 6:10-18)
(e.g., maternity clothes and accessories)

I.   **Hat**
(The Helmet of Salvation)

II.   **Shirt/Blouse**
(The Breastplate of Righteousness)

III.   **Bullet Proof Vest**
(The Shield of Faith)

IV.   **Belt for Your Pants or Skirt**
(The Belt of Truth)

V.   **Gun or Knife**
(The Sword of the Spirit)

VI.   **Shoes**
(The Gospel of Peace)

VII.   **The Code Language**
(Pray always in the Spirit)

VIII.   **The Spiritual Voucher for the Maternity Clothes**
(Check your love walk)

Spiritual Maternity Clothes & Accessories

D id you know that even though you may have accepted the Lord as your personal Lord and Savior, it is possible for you not to be in the will of God? Did you know that giving your life to God by accepting Jesus Christ as your personal Lord and Savior is only one part of your obligation? You must also commit to *True Purpose* for your life so that you can begin the mission that you signed up for when you invited God into your life.

Imagine signing up for a movement but you're refusing to take a stand against opposition that may come as a result of your position in the movement. Not too long ago I read an article in The Oprah Magazine, "The Freedom Riders". Some Human Rights Crusaders that made it through a Civil Rights Movement held in Jackson, Mississippi stood against great opposition at that time.

Prior to signing up for this movement, the activists were aware of the opposition they would face. Nonetheless, it did not deter them from moving forward and openly announcing their position which also included "jail, no bail" as a part of their strategy for action. In this movement there were some casualties and survivors that lived to tell their story. Like the Civil Rights Movement led by Dr. Martin Luther King, Jr., was ignited as a result of the late Rosa Parks taking a stand in Alabama, these individuals that lived through the Civil Rights Movement in Jackson also took a stand for their belief. One young lady stated, "You can kill my body, but you can't kill my soul." This is the type of stand that God wants from us with regards to the Movement that Jesus Christ started when He was here. The movement of spiritual equality, love, hope, peace, freedom, and power all available through God (the higher power) as you allow yourself to be guided by the Holy Spirit (the Spirit of God – the higher power).

Imagine signing up for a movement but you're refusing to take a stand against opposition that may come as a result of your position in the movement.

As a child of God, you signed up for the "Christ Movement". In this "Christ Movement" you will face persecution naturally and spiritually. According to Romans 8:17, to share in the glory of Jesus Christ, you must share in the suffering of Jesus Christ. According to Ephesians 6:13: *"You wrestle not against flesh and blood, but against principalities and the rulers of darkness."* Yes, you are in the flesh, but this means that you will come to know the greater battle, which is in the spirit. You conquer the spirit, you automatically conquer the flesh – you conquer life! You have such the upper hand on life when you operate and control in the spirit realm.

To accept Jesus as your personal Lord and Savior as your leader in this "Christ Movement" without implementing *True Purpose* in your life is like going to war and not fighting, or joining a Movement and not taking a stand in the Movement, less alone having an understanding as to why you joined the Movement. Or if you're in a war, it's like not knowing what to do on the battlefield. To do this, would make you a wandering soldier – wondering around aimlessly (completely clueless) in battle. Imagine that – pretty ridiculous, huh?

What is sure to happen to a wondering soldier, without the proper training (I'll call him Jim)? I'm sure you could guess…If Jim doesn't die early, Jim will not be of any benefit to the team, and the likelihood of Jim coming out of the war victoriously is slim. It is almost guaranteed that Jim won't be able to stand for long, and if he does, his fight will more than likely be harder because he's clueless. He doesn't know how to use his gear and he has no knowledge of the enemy's techniques that I'm sure he would have learned about if he had received proper training and received understanding of his position. This is not a good visual is it? So, you must complete the "Yes" by submitting to the call of God – the *True Purpose* for your life, then you must receive proper training for the "Christ Movement" – the spiritual battle for which you've signed up.

God admonishes us in Ephesians 6:11 to put on the whole Armor of God so that we can stand against the wiles of the enemy. When you complete your "Yes", the enemy will say, "It is on"! Therefore, in order to make it through this spiritual pregnancy, it will be very important for you to know who you are in God (your strength and authority on the battlefield). You need to be completely geared up for battle. If not, you will stand the chance of aborting what God has planted inside of you as a result of ignorance concerning spiritual warfare. Therefore, to prevent spiritual abortion of ***True Purpose*** for your life, you must understand how to apply the Armor of God (Ephesians 6:10-18) to your life. Additionally, you must walk in Love or it is all pointless! *"And if I have prophetic powers (the gift of interpreting the divine will and purpose), and understand all the secret truths and mysteries and possess all knowledge, and if I have [sufficient] faith so that I can remove mountains, but have not love (God's love in me) I am nothing (a useless nobody)"* (I Corinthians 13:1-3).

Get ready to get properly dressed for this spiritual pregnancy and learn how the "Armor of God" and Spiritual Pregnancy relate to this blind and intangible experience. Very essential!

The Hat (The Helmet of Salvation)

And take the helmet of salvation... (Ephesians 6:17)

Know who you are in God! Webster's dictionary defines *salvation* as: "Deliverance from destruction, difficulty or evil; deliverance from the power or penalty of sin; redemption; to be rescued." In war, the helmet is used to shield your head from the darts or bullets shot from the enemy. In the spirit realm, you are to wear this helmet of "salvation" so that you will be shielded from the enemies' attacks on your head (your mind, will, and emotions), which he will attack by planting seeds of doubt regarding your position in God (e.g., confusion, worthiness), so that you will abort your spiritual pregnancy.

According to Psalm 27:1, *"THE LORD is my Light and my Salvation—whom shall I fear or dread? The Lord is the Refuge and Stronghold of my life—of whom shall I be afraid?"* So if the Lord is your strength, the enemy can't defeat you. Not to mention, God has already mapped out the plans for your life (Ephesians 2:10). Therefore, all you need to know is in whom you trust and believe and it will come to pass, just like it did for Mary (Matthew 9:29)! God said that His word will not return unto Him void (Isaiah 55:11)! Therefore, if God said it, that settles it!

Due to the necessity for you to be completely guided by the Holy Spirit during this spiritual process the enemy will try to attack your mind with confusion, as well as doubt, fear, and unbelief. The enemy will place doubts in your mind regarding your intellect and your ability, etc. Nevertheless, you must know that it is not by your might but by God's might do you operate (Acts 1:8). You are completely guided by the Spirit (Romans 8:4-5, Galatians 5:16). Your strength comes from God (Psalm 18:32; 27:1; 28:7), and God is not the author confusion (I Corinthians 14:33).

The American Heritage Dictionary defines *confuse* as: "1. To cause to be unable to think with clarity, or act with intelligence or understanding... 2c. To assemble without order or sense; jumble." OK, being that our God is all knowing, omnipotent, and with all power, confusion is contrary to who God is. God is not ignorant, short of intellect, understanding or clarity, unorganized or jumbled. Therefore, considering that you are operating under the power of the Holy Spirit (His power, His knowing, His guidance, His might); confusion has no place in your mind! The enemy has NO POWER! Glory to God!

Pray this prayer:

> *"I take authority as God has given me in Matthew 16:19,*
> *that whatsoever I bind on earth is bound in heaven and*
> *whatsoever I loose on earth is loosed in heaven. Satan,*

according to Matthew 16:19, I bind you and your worker Confusion up in the name of Jesus! According to Matthew 16:19, I loose the spirit of God in me NOW according to Jeremiah 51:15! In the Name of Jesus, I cast the spirit of confusion into the abyss NOW!"

Now praise and give thanks to God for giving you the attributes of the Holy Spirit! Worship Him for He is all powerful, all knowing and He is an Awesome God! Know that God is the source of your strength.

Shirt or Blouse (The Breastplate of Righteousness)

Stand therefore...and having on the breastplate of righteousness (Ephesians 6:14).

The Roman soldiers wore the breastplate to protect the upper body. As a child of God you must be sure to put on the "Breastplate of Righteousness" so that you can protect your upper body as well; mainly your heart! In your heart you must know who you are as a result of the sacrifice of Jesus Christ so that you can confidently go about your life as God has instructed of you and without condemnation. Understanding that "Righteousness" is through Jesus Christ is crucial so that you do not fall prey to the spirit of condemnation. Again, the lack of understanding of righteousness causes you to question your worthiness of the call of God on your life. Vine's Expository Dictionary of New Testament Words defines righteousness as "The gracious gift of God to men whereby all who believe on the Lord Jesus Christ are brought into right relationship with God. This righteousness is unattainable by obedience to any law, or by any merit of man's own, or any other condition than that of faith in Christ."

I must admit, when I wrote my first book, The Armor of God, I had no clue as to what to write regarding the "Breastplate of Righteousness." The Holy Spirit had to guide me to the verses in the bible to read regarding this because I was clueless. As a result of my beliefs as a child, this revelation had to grow on me. I couldn't grasp the concept of "righteous through Christ" not being about "my" works. Again, this means once saved, always saved. Once you're a child of God, you're always a child of God and God let's us know that very clearly in His word (Galatians 5:17-18).

I remember the first time that I fell out of fellowship with God. I was 21 years old and I was living with my then boyfriend, now ex-husband. I couldn't explain how quickly I went from the good little "church girl" to "the church girl shacking with her man" as many would label me back then. I was really going along with the guidelines set forth by the church and considered my self as a young lady that practiced what she preached. Anyhow, I became so condemned for my lifestyle at the time that I stopped my usual conversations with God for about 2 years. I wished I had an umbrella to just hide myself from God. I was embarrassed and sad that I had lost the relationship I once had with God.

At that time I admired a young lady at work for always reading the bible everyday at lunch. I longed to have the relationship with God that she seemed to have; but, I figured that it wouldn't make since because I didn't have the strength to stop the lifestyle I had begun. Well, one day I approached the young lady and my first words to her were, "I used to be saved". What she said to me began to change my life, but I was confused and in denial at first. She looked up at me as she stopped reading the Bible for a moment, and questioned me, "Use to be saved?" I answered, "Yes, I used to, but I live with my boyfriend."

As I recall how I felt in my heart at that time, tears fall from my eyes. I would hate for someone to feel like I did. I felt so lonely. I felt that I was just doomed to hell. I felt that God was ashamed and disappointed in me. I felt that I couldn't talk to anybody. The church didn't understand what I was going through and I was told to just stop living with my boyfriend and that I should know better. I was also told that I was no longer a child of God. Yet, in spite of my beliefs at that time, it wasn't that simple to leave. I loved my ex-husband (then boyfriend), we had a son, and I didn't want to be a statistic. Therefore, I was judged for my decision to stay. So, my Christian friends judged me and my worldly friends condoned me. The most disturbing of all was that based on my beliefs at that time, I thought I wasn't God's child anymore and that hurt me more than anything!

The young lady then asked me, "Don't you have a son?" I answered, "Yes." She then asked me, "If your son became a mass murderer, would you want him to be executed?" I adamantly answered, "No, that's my son! I mean, I would realize that what he

> As I recall how I felt in my heart at that time, tears fall from my eyes. I would hate for someone to feel like I did. I felt so lonely. I felt that I was just doomed to hell.

had done was wrong, so I would want him to get help and he would deserve jail, but not death. That's my son!" She asked me, "If you love your son like that and you're of the flesh, how much more do you think God loves you?" She went on further to say, "You are not even capable of loving like God loves." She then showed me in the word that I was still a child of God no matter what – regardless of my works (Galatians 5:4-8; 17-18). She told me that God was just waiting to hear from me and that He never left me. She said that I was still His child. Wow! She gave me so much hope that day.

I then went home and I talked to God whom I perceive as my Heavenly Father, on a personal note. I remember sitting on my living room floor and recalling the conversation that I had with the young lady that day. So, I said to God, "Hi – I miss you," as I cried before the Lord for strength and guidance. I then began thanking God for His mercy and grace in my life. The Holy Spirit spoke back to me, "Hi". I'll never forget that moment and how I felt. It was from that moment I built my relationship with God from a different perspective – based on "LOVE", "not condemnation" or "fear of Hell". I thank God for the revelation of the Holy Spirit because when I couldn't turn to even the "church" without just dropping my lifestyle, God's Spirit came and took over me, positioning me for a complete change in my life. That's when I turned back to God and allowed Him to reveal to me who He was without man's interpretation or views and it has been AWESOME! It is great to be free (Galatians 5:1)!

Again, by faith, you have to believe that you have been made the righteousness of God through Jesus Christ, so the enemy can not challenge who you are in Christ or your worthiness of spiritual pregnancy (Romans 3:22-27). Through the sacrifice that Jesus made, and that alone, are you worthy! Therefore, do not focus on your faults, rather, be obedient and follow God's plan that He's already planned for you (Ephesians 2:10). If you sin, repent and move on. According to I John 1:9, "If you confess your sins, He is faithful and just to forgive you of your sins and to cleanse you from all unrighteousness." **Remember:** to live a righteous life is to live like Jesus did: completely guided by the Holy Spirit (Romans 8:4)!

Receive what God gives you in confidence at whatever point you are in your life by Faith. Through your gift you will find deliverance!

Bullet-Proof Vest (The Shield of Faith)

Above all, taking the shield of faith, where with ye shall be able to quench all the fiery darts of the wicked (Ephesians 6:16).

The Roman soldiers included a shield to stop the arrows of the enemy from reaching and injuring them. The Shield of Faith is also a vital part of your spiritual Armor. It protects you from the fiery darts the enemy hurls your way (Ephesians 6:16). In this process, the enemy will place an attack on your mind, your peace, challenge what you believe, tempt you to speak against what you "believe" the Lord is promising you, try to distract you from the Word of God because he knows that your weapon in the battle is the Sword – the Word of God; challenge your Love walk (e.g., judging people), you name it, the enemy is coming with an attack on any area you could possibly imagine. After all, the last thing the enemy would like to see is for you to make it to a "fulfilled" life! Therefore, you can't afford to not have your shield of faith in position at all times! Shields UP!

The Lord is taking you out of your comfort zone and placing you in a position where it is necessary for you to trust Him completely, listen for His voice before you move, etc. You must have your shield up at all times in this era. You must believe in what you don't see, you must believe in *True Purpose* for your life. The Bible reads in Hebrews 11:1, "*Now, faith is the substance of things hoped for, the evidence of things not seen.*" Also, according to Hebrews 11:6: "*But without faith it is **impossible** to please Him: for He that cometh to God must believe that He is and that He is a rewarder of them that diligently seek Him.*"

He tells you in Philippians 4:13 that you can do "all things" through Christ that strengthens you! This can not be done without the power of God in your life. In Him is where your Faith must stand!

Imagine you and the enemy at war and you're attempting to complete out the mission that God has instructed of you. One likely spot the enemy will attack is your mind, "You're a fool." "You know that you can't do this." "You can't go speak to that executive, they'll turn you away," and God only knows whatever else he will bring to your mind. How do you use your shield in this instance?

> Receive what God gives you in confidence at whatever point you are in your life by Faith. Through your gift you will find deliverance!

Faith without works is dead (James 2:20, 26). A great

example of action is opening your mouth and confessing what God has spoken to you aloud. Proclaim through praise and thanksgiving, what God has promised you, just like Mary did.

A wonderful example of PRAISE is giving THANKS for the promise... "Lord, I praise you for you are worthy to be praised! Father, I th*ank you for what you are doing and have already called to be so! I believe and trust the Word you've given me! Glory to God!"* (Unless God has instructed you to be quiet on the specifics, call out what God has promised).

Faith is an action word and this spiritual pregnancy is a blind, non-tangible walk of faith; unlike in a natural pregnancy. Your faith will be tried time and time again until delivery, and it gets worse the closer you are to the manifestation of *True Purpose* being implemented in your life. So it is important that you remain strong in your faith and continue to push towards the mark of the high calling of Jesus Christ with ALL THAT YOU HAVE (Philippians 3:14)! Know that NO WEAPON formed against you shall prosper and God has spoken in His word that you can do all things through Christ that strengthens you (Isaiah 54:17, Philippians 4:13). Remind yourself of your weapons in this spiritual pregnancy, which is the WORD OF GOD, the Sword. So, when the enemy begins to throw the darts your way to break your stand, stab him with the "SWORD" - THE WORD OF GOD and stand in Faith that your weapons are effective to defend you in any situation!

When fighting, it is natural to raise your hands or to put something in front of you as a defense. Other options would be to run, to fall flat on your face, or to dodge behind something without fighting back out of fear. Due to your signs of weakness, if you did something like this in a natural war, your own team would probably turn against you. Or, the Commander in Chief would definitely move you from the front-line or even the war. You would have some consequences to pay for your actions.

In the spirit realm, God has provided us with all of the tools to fight and the shield of faith which is your hope in believing what is not tangible. God says that he has not given us the spirit of fear, but of love, power, and a sound mind, so whom shall you fear (II Timothy 1:7)! You are to be wise and strategic on the battlefield, and you are to utilize your shield as protection from the darts that will be thrown your way. Think about it, if you were in a war and you were given a shield that you can shift around to protect yourself from being wounded, to not use it would be crazy!

You must walk in faith and maintain your joy as you go through what is necessary in order for you to deliver *True Purpose* in your life. You must also walk in love so that you may even utilize the shield of faith effectively. We are taught in the Word of God, the only thing that counts is faith which expresses itself through love (Galatians 5:6). So, without love your faith doesn't operate, like without gas your car doesn't run.

You can not fulfill the call of God in your life without LOVE because without love your faith is pointless. For the lack of love you will remain a wandering and confused person in life. Never knowing which direction you're headed or getting places and never being totally fulfilled. More bluntly, according to the Holy Bible, without love you are NOTHING and you are a useless body (I Corinthians 13:1-3)! A little harsh? Not really. God is Love and if you profess to be a child of God, you are to also be love! Otherwise, your life will not operate how God planned it for you. In fact, it is an insult to profess to be a child of God and not operate in love.

So, by faith which works by love and that alone will you make it through this spiritual pregnancy successfully. You must know going into this that you will DELIVER no matter what and you will stand firm on your faith and walk in love! When the enemy comes to attack you, use the Word of God and shield of faith simultaneously. Wherever the enemy goes to attack, put your faith in that area by putting the shield of faith up and proclaiming the Word of God! If God says it, that settles it (Isaiah 55:11)!

Belt for your Pants or Skirt (The Belt of Truth)

Stand therefore, having your loins girt about with truth... (Ephesians 6:14)

The belt referred to in this scripture, for the Roman soldiers, covered a gap where the joints of the armor joined together. The Roman soldier wore a strong piece of armor around his waist. This protected his stomach and other organs. "Having your loins girt" means having the belt around your waist buckled. What would happen if you had on loose pants or a skirt and the belt around your waist wasn't buckled? You would lose your skirt or pants. Not a good scene because you are then exposed. That's the way it is in the Spirit realm when you do not have the "Belt of Truth" on. You have exposed yourself to the attacks of the enemy.

According to Random House Dictionary loins is defined as: "3a. the parts of the body between the hips and the lower ribs, esp. regarded as the seat of physical strength and 'generative' power."

Therefore, loins being the seat of strength for the body lets us know that this is a very key part that holds the body together. God says that you are to "have your loins", which the word "your" indicates that you already have the loins (your: the possessive form of you), which also means that you already have the power to or **function of propagating or reproducing** (generative power). According to Random House Dictionary *generative* is defined as: "1. capable of producing or creating 2. pertaining to the production of offspring." As for the way the bible uses the word "girt", the American Heritage College Dictionary

> God is also saying that you have the power to produce or create pertaining to the production of offspring (your spiritual gift).

describes girt as: "1. to gird." The same Dictionary defines gird as: "3. To prepare (oneself) for action: *To summon up one's inner resources in preparation for action.*" Random House Dictionary defines **gird** as: "to prepare oneself for something requiring readiness, strength, and endurance: *He girded his loins to face his competitor.*" **Summary**: *The "Belt of Truth is Crucial to this battle!"*

Just in understanding how the dictionary describes the words that the Lord gave us, you can receive a deeper revelation of "The Belt of Truth". God says that you are required to prepare. You must be physically strengthened and ready for endurance – "having your loins girt about with truth…" God is also saying that you have the power to produce or create pertaining to the production of offspring (your spiritual gift). However, in order for the power to manifest in your life, you must recognize that your strength lies in THE TRUTH!!

The American Heritage College Dictionary defines *truth* as: "1. Conformity to fact or actuality. 2. A statement proven to be or accepted as fact or actuality."

What are some facts that are proven to be accepted or actuality concerning God?

1. God is the Higher Power that has shown Himself to be Almighty, Faithful, and Powerful (Revelation 4:8).
2. God is a God of freedom and has afforded us free will (Romans 8:21, I Peter 2:16).
3. God is not a God of condemnation (I Corinthians 6:11; Romans 3:24; Ephesians 2:8; Romans 8:1).
4. God is Love (John 3:16; Romans 5:8; Romans 5:11).
5. God's Word will not return unto Him void and He's not a God that He should lie (Numbers 23:19; Isaiah 55:11).
6. God is your strength (Psalm 27:1; 28:7)

NOTE: I must also mention that I now understand and believe as the Spirit leads me that because some of you may choose to stumble on the gender or the difference of perception, "God" is who "God" is and that's all that matters. God may, or may not be a man, but I choose to refer to the Heavenly God, the higher power, the omnipotent as a "He", as my Heavenly "Father" in my life and I'm sure many of you view God the same. Be free to know God for who God is in your life, so long as you know that God is the higher power, the omnipotent, the love we all desire, the peace, the joy, the freedom, and above "God" there is no other. Another great fact about God is that He chooses to share His love and His power through us so that He can work together with us.

Tools for Truth

God has given us the written Word of God (The Holy Bible) as our main tool to reference for truths concerning Him. Although often misinterpreted and taken out of context, if you seek guidance from the Holy Spirit and not man, He will give you the right interpretation of the Word of God as it pertains to your life. The Holy Spirit will guide you and teach you all things if you ask Him, including the truth regarding the Holy Bible (John 14:26). I dare you to ask Him.

There may be many of you that believe there are other powerful spiritual sources in addition to the Holy Bible. Although, I do believe that may be true; I firmly believe the Holy Bible is the foundation of it all. As God used the writers of the Holy Bible, He continues to use Authors today so that the Word of God is continuous as they too are led by the Spirit.

Consider this: The Holy Bible is the most powerful weapon that you have in your collection of war guns. No other weapon that you have will defeat the enemy like the ammunition from the Holy Bible. So, it behooves you to have wisdom and understanding of how to use the most powerful weapon in your gun collection.

In addition to the written Word of God, you are required to also stand on the Voice of God, the guidance of the Holy Spirit (some of you may refer to the Spirit of God as your God Consciousness). Personally, I am led by the Holy Spirit and I'm not a BIBLE SCHOLAR. However, the Holy Spirit leads and guides me and often times guides me through the Holy Bible as a confirmation of what He's given me in the Spirit.

The Word of God as it is written in the Holy Bible is what I know to be proven fact. The Word of God is rich; it will never fail you and you can cross reference the foundation of whatever the Holy Spirit leads you to do or confirms to you regarding the core of God in the scriptures.

God needs you to stand on His Word (verbal or written). He needs you to know that just as He's using me to write this book, He's used others to write, including the Holy Bible while under the influence of the Holy Spirit (Galatians 5:16)! So you must be careful not to speak against the written Word of God (The Holy Bible), so that you are not guilty of speaking against the work of the Holy Spirit. If you don't understand, BE QUIET! Keep your mouth off of God and His Word from wherever or however it comes! Again, I dare you to ask the Holy Spirit to give you revelation of His Word (written or spoken).

I did not plan to write the last three paragraphs (OK…Holy Spirit!). Let's continue with Truth. You must know that there is *no other god*, but God, the **Almighty**, Powerful and Omnipotent (Exodus 20:3)! According to Exodus 34:14: "For you shall worship no other god; for the Lord, Whose name is Jealous, is a jealous (*impassioned*) God." I'd like to define **impassioned**, which is the translation of "jealous" in this scripture according to the Amplified Version of the Bible. According to the American Heritage Dictionary, impassioned is defined as: "Full of passion; fervent." Passionate is defined as: "1. Having or showing strong feelings; full of passion." "3. resulting from, expressing, or tending to arouse strong feeling; ardent; intense; impassioned." In the same Dictionary, fervent is defined as: "1. Having or showing great emotion or zeal…" "2.

Having or showing great warmth of feeling, intensely devoted or earnest." Our Father is passionate and fervent towards His children. He is a God of Love not **"Jealousy"** as defined in the American Heritage Dictionary today or as interpreted via the translation in many versions of the Holy Bible.

The American Heritage Dictionary defines jealous: "Fearful or wary of being supplanted; apprehensive of losing affection or position. Resentful, or bitter in rivalry; envious." Jealousy, as defined here is contrary to what the Word of God teaches us about our Heavenly Father or what you will learn through your "personal relationship" with Him. Our Heavenly Father is not capable of these attributes. He is a God of Love (John 3:16)! In the Amplified version, jealousy is translated for us as impassioned. Unfortunately, this has been misinterpreted by many. As you see, it is very crucial when you are reading the Word of God that you study and seek counsel from the Holy Spirit for interpretation. You must correctly analyze so that you can rightfully interpret the Word of God which may include using other reference materials (2 Timothy 2:15)! Therefore, to have no other god before Him means that in Him and in Him alone should you rely on for your strength (Psalm 27:1; 28:7).

God is Almighty, Powerful, and Faithful

The American Heritage College Dictionary defines Almighty as: "having absolute power." **Absolute** is defined as: "to be perfect in quality; not limited by restrictions or exceptions; unconditional; not to be doubted or questioned; positive." Wow!! This means that

God's power is perfect in quality, has no restrictions or exceptions. It is unconditional and NOT TO BE DOUBTED OR QUESTIONED! Regardless of your situation He is powerful. Revelation 1:8 reads, *"I am Alpha and Omega, the beginning and the ending, saith the Lord, which is, which was, and which is to come, the Almighty."*

God is faithful, glory to God! The American Heritage College Dictionary defines **Faithful** as: "1. Adhering firmly and devotedly, as to a person or an idea; loyal; worthy of trust or belief; reliable." *"God is faithful, by whom you were called unto the fellowship of his Son Jesus Christ our Lord* (I Corinthians 1:9)." Read this powerful scripture, Deuteronomy 32:4: "He is the Rock; His work is perfect, for all His ways are law and justice. A God of faithfulness **without breach or deviation**, just and right is He." Well, Glory to God to the Most High!

During your spiritual pregnancy, know that God is faithful and He will not tempt you above that which you're able to bear (I Corinthians 10:13). He will guard you from evil as it is written in II Thessalonians 3:3. Therefore, you should not waver regardless of what you face during this spiritual pregnancy (Hebrews 10:23)! Just know that He will guard you from evil.

Well glory! What is your "hope" in this spiritual pregnancy transition in life? That you are protected and guarded from evil! You have the VICTORY! In II Thessalonians 3:3 you are reminded that in His faithfulness to us, He will strengthen and guard you from evil. Since that's the case, what is there to fear with the Lord on your side? This is Truth!

The Enemy has NO POWER!

Now that you should be clearly aware of the victorious side, let's look at the truth about the opposing side. The enemy can not stand up against the Word of God when spoken from someone who has the Power of the Holy Spirit within them (Acts 1:8, 10:38; Romans 8:13)! The enemy knows that there are many people who proclaim to walk in the Spirit and will utter mere words at him while attempting to stop him in his tracks. However, if you are not walking in the Spirit, you have no power. You have no weight! Nevertheless, through the authority that you have through the power of God, made

...through the authority that you have through the power of God, made available through the righteousness of Jesus Christ, you have POWER to defeat the enemy on any level (I Corinthians 6:14)!

available through the righteousness of Jesus Christ, you have POWER to defeat the enemy on any level (I Corinthians 6:14)!

According to Mark 3:26, *"And if Satan rise up against himself, and be divided, he can not stand, but hath an end."* According to Luke 11:17-18: *"...any kingdom divided against itself is laid waste; and a house divided against itself falls. If Satan also is divided against himself, how will his kingdom stand...?"* The enemy is VOID of POWER! He is laid waste and he can not stand!

Stop giving "Satan" more recognition than deserved. You must understand that the enemy is void of power! Satan can only do what he is allowed to do. In most cases, many attacks from the enemy are due to the lack of knowledge that many of you have with regards to spiritual warfare. It is your responsibility to gain an understanding of how to properly battle the enemy during this intangible process. (Also read Chapter 6)

Just something to think about...

If you lived on a battle field, you would probably sleep with a grenade or shot gun in your hand. You would probably never leave the house unarmed as a precaution of being caught off guard by the enemy. Why would you think anything different spiritually? The Lord guides us through His Word as to how we are to protect ourselves from the enemy. He admonishes us to PUT ON THE FULL ARMOR OF GOD so that we may be able stand against the wiles of the enemy (Ephesians 6:11)! He said that we wrestle not against flesh and blood, but against the principalities and the rulers of darkness (Ephesians 6:10)! So, how can anyone live without putting on the Full Armor of God? I couldn't think of a worse war than one that I must fight blind folded (the fight is intangible - you can't touch your opponent). How much more should you be prepared?

Gun or Knife (The Sword of the Spirit)

And take the helmet of salvation, the sword of the Spirit, which is the Word of God...(Ephesians 6:17)

To complete the armor of the Roman soldiers, they carried a sword, but it was not just any type of sword. The Greek word for sword in this Scripture is "machaira." The design of this sword is very different from other swords carried back in that time of history. It was only 18-inches long, pretty short when compared to other swords. Not only did it have a sharp point, but also both sides of the blade were sharp. The sword was very light, so it didn't throw the Roman soldier off balance. Roman soldiers won great victories with this sword.

The Word of God is a "machaira", a sword that does not leave you off balance. Instead, when handled skillfully, it will defeat the enemy every time, praise God! The scripture describes the Word of God as a **two-edged** sword.

For the Word of God is quick, and powerful, and sharper than any two-edged sword, piercing even to the dividing asunder of soul and spirit, and of the joints and marrow, and is a discerner of the thoughts and intents of the heart. (Hebrews 4:12)

Glory to God! The Word of God is quick, **powerful**, and sharper than any two-edged sword. Vine's Complete Expository Dictionary of Old and New Testament Words defines quicken as: "to make alive, cause to live." It takes its root from "Zoe", the Greek word that means "life as God has it; life in the absolute sense." When you confess the Word of God in the name or authority of Jesus, there is power! (Acts 4:10, Acts 4:28-30). Vine's defines powerful as: "**active**, strong, and mighty."

Vine's defines active as: "in work; active". According to The American College Heritage, active means: "being in physical motion; disposed to take action or to effectuate change; being in continuous use or in a state of action." Wow! The "Word of God – the sword" is a book of verbs or action words. The Word of God is meant to effectuate change, because the Word of God is active. The Word of God is to be used continuously in our lives with physical exertion. It can't be manifested if you don't EXERT IT! The part I really love is the "expressing action rather than a state of being." The Word of God is there for you to use, and we all know it. However, the question is: "Are you utilizing it as a state of being or action in your life?"

The Word of God must be used daily for you are consistently wrestling against principalities and the rulers of darkness (Ephesians 6:12). However, you don't have to experience defeat in your life if you take the Sword and properly clothe yourself with the rest of your spiritual armor daily (Ephesians 6:13). Yes, you will experience tests that are only to make you stronger, giving you strength to graduate *to the next level* (closer to a life of TOTAL fulfillment), but you don't have to experience defeat time and time again in your life.

> Yes, you will experience tests that are only to make you stronger...but you don't have to experience defeat time and time again in your life.

The Bible says that life and death are in the power of the tongue (Proverbs 18:21). What comes off of the tongue? Words... So that you activate the proper words off of your tongue, know what the Word of God says about your spiritual pregnancy. Know how to get TOTAL VICTORY in your life through the POWER of the WORD OF GOD that is spoken out of your mouth!

OK...Ready to get ACTIVE in the Word of God?

Even Jesus used the Word of God when He was tested by the enemy and God expects us to do the same (Matthew 4:7)! In this spiritual pregnancy, the enemy is going to be working overtime in attempts to cause you to abort your spiritual pregnancy. Therefore, you cannot hesitate to draw your sword, the Word of God.

Imagine being on the battlefield and the enemy is coming towards you with his weapon. Will you freeze up or will you quickly draw the weapon that God has equipped you with? As the ole cliché goes: "you snooze, you lose!" Just as in a natural war, being too slow to draw your weapon can cost you your life. In the spirit realm, being too slow to draw your weapon (the Word of God) can cost you your spiritual pregnancy. The enemy will consider that a weakness and use that lack of knowledge that you apparently have to his advantage. He will then hit you where it really hurts and try to put a jabber in you that a surgeon wouldn't be able to pull out. I HATE THE ENEMY! Don't give him the upper hand in your life!

Not having the Word of God embedded in your heart and mind is like being on the battlefield without any weapons. Crazy? So don't be caught standing on the front-line with the enemy in your face and you standing there with no confidence to use your spiritual weapon to fight back because you haven't had the training (you haven't studied the Word of God, nor have you spent time with God to hear what He's saying to you). When you spend time with God (the Holy Spirit) daily, and in His Word (the Word of God), you are abiding in Him. If you abide in the Lord, you will bring forth the fruit of victory every time! In John 15:7-8, God gives you a powerful directive:

If you abide in me, and my Word abides in you, ye shall ask what ye will, and it shall be done unto you. Herein is my Father glorified, that ye bear much fruit; so shall ye be my disciples.

Every time you confess the Word of God over your situation, you are using your "machaira" and cutting the enemy with it. You are to patiently face your trials, and use your confessions of the Word of God strong and consistently, and the devil will leave you, just like Satan left Jesus (Matthew 4:10-11). The enemy knows that he's defeated; however, he is going to see how far he can take you before "you realize" that he's defeated. How will he know? The evidence of you properly using the tools you have. He didn't stop tempting Jesus after the first time Jesus used the Word of God on him. The enemy tested Jesus three times alone in this verse of scripture (Matthew 4: 3-11). The Holy Spirit led Jesus into the wilderness to be tempted by Satan (Matthew 4:1). God had Jesus serve as yet another example: 1) You are to be patient and consistent in your stand on the Word of God regardless of how many times or different ways the enemy attacks you. Power, patience, and consistency will bring results! Continue to stand on the Word of God and the enemy will flee!

I love this revelation of the ***Armor of God***! Put the Word to use in your life and watch it take a change in the direction God planned for it to go. That's right. Start stabbing the enemy and his entourage (his team) with the Sword (the Word of God) and the enemy will flee!

This is an Effective Spiritual Warfare Prayer...

Lord, according to John 15:7, You said that if I abide in You and Your Word abides in me, that I shall ask what I will and it shall be done. In Matthew 16:19 You said that whatsoever I bind on earth it shall be bound in heaven and whatsoever I loose on earth it shall be loosed in heaven. So, according to your Word, I take authority over this situation and I bind up the spirit of (e.g., deceit) and I loose the spirit of (e.g., truth). Lord in Isaiah 55:11, You said that Your word would not return unto me void. I take the authority that You've given me over my life and I bind Satan and this spirit of (e.g., deceit) from the root and I cast them into the abyss! Lord, I stand on your word that I am free in the name of Jesus! No weapon formed against me shall prosper as you said in your word, (Isaiah 55:11)! Glory to God! Lord, I praise you and I lift you high above all the earth!

To Summarize: Sharpen your sword daily by meditating on the Word of God (e.g., Scriptures in the Holy Bible, His directives to you) and spending time with God so that you may hear what God is saying to you regarding your spiritual pregnancy. The more time you spend with God, the more sensitive your spirit will become to the voice of the Lord and you will receive a much greater revelation with regards to His written Word. Whatever situation you are up against, you must use the Word of God to attack the enemy when he challenges the Word that God has given you, rather written or spoken. Meditate on the written Word so that when the attacks come, you can quickly jab the enemy with God's written Word just as Jesus did (Matthew 4:7)!

Shoes (The Gospel of Peace)

And your feet shod with the preparation of the gospel of peace...(Ephesians 6:15).

Roman soldiers wore heavy foot gear. The bottom of their sandals had nails attached to the soles, which made them sure-footed and able to stand strong in battle. Due to the intangible nature of this pregnancy, the enemy uses the mind to plant seeds of doubt, which brings about restlessness and anxiety, and causes you to lose focus (lose balance on the battlefield) and confidence. However, you must find rest in God - peace (Joshua 1:13; Job 25:2; Romans 15:13). He has already given you VICTORY (I Corinthians 15:57)! Furthermore, God admonishes us not to fret (not be uneasy) nor to have anxiety (uncertainty, fear…) for nothing and you will see the PEACE of God, which passes all understanding (Philippians 4:6-7).

Be confident in knowing that what God has called in your life will come to pass regardless of what you go through. Know that whatever you go through is just a part of the process. Before God appointed you for the specific purpose in your life, He already knew what you were going to do. Therefore, if you go astray from what God has instructed you to do, repent and move on (I John 1:9). According to Psalm 103:12: *"God is faithful and just to forgive your transgressions as far is the east is from the west."* So, do not waddle in your mistake. If God has forgotten it, you forget it, move on and intend to sin no more!

PAUSE: Some people ask the question, "If Jesus Christ has already died for our sins, why do I have to repent for any sin?" I understand your position. As I've prayed for the answer to this often asked questioned, this is what I have to give to you. It is not complicated. Think of life. If you do something in error to someone you love here on earth, wouldn't you apologize for what you've done as a symbol of remorse for how you've wronged them? Otherwise, your loved one may feel used or abused because you've shown no sign of remorse for your actions. Although God knows your heart, this is a relationship that we are talking about in conjunction with a life of fulfillment, and living as an example for who God is and the sacrifice of Jesus Christ for your life. God is love and if you love God there should be remorse for your actions that you know hurt your Father.

I know that you may feel at times that you've completely messed up what God has planned for you as a result of a mistake or disobedient act you may possibly do or may have done. STOP! We're going to pause right here for another moment for those that are under attack in this area to take action right now against the enemy… *Bind up the Spirit of Doubt, Fear, and Unbelief and loose Truth, Love, Power, and a Sound Mind according to (2 Timothy 1:7); Bind up the Spirit of Condemnation and loose the Spirit of Righteousness; Bind up the Spirit of Disobedience and Loose the Spirit of Obedience! In the Name of Jesus! After you complete binding and loosing, begin to Praise God! For His mercy and grace endures forever! Praise and thank God for His forgiveness! I almost forgot, the enemy will definitely try to bring you down emotionally, so, Bind up the spirit of Depression and Loose Joy! For the Joy of the Lord is your Strength according to Nehemiah 8:10!* OK, let's move on...

Just because you're spiritually pregnant doesn't mean that you have to be perfect while carrying. The whole point of this pregnancy, besides getting you in right position on this earth, is to

...you must recognize that in order to graduate to any level, there will be tests, and sometimes you just might fail.

build your faith and confidence in God so that you may understand that through God's ability in you, all things are possible (Romans 8:28)! Therefore, you must recognize that in order to graduate to any level, there will be tests, and sometimes you just might fail. If you do, through the strength of God, GET BACK UP!

Unless you disobey the call of God, you should stand in everything you do with the Peace of God (confidence) that everything is going to work out according to God's plan, so that you may fulfill *True Purpose* in your life!

Simply Stated:

PEACE = Obedience: Confidence, Power, Authority, Rest, and of the like
NO PEACE = Disobedience: Confusion, Insecurity, Doubt, Fear, Unbelief, Restlessness and of the like

I Corinthians 2:5: *"...that your faith might not rest in the wisdom of men but in the power of God."* Again, your faith comes from having faith in the power of God! Let go of worry and fear and replace it with faith, patience and confidence. This is completely attainable by implementing *True Purpose* in your life! Stand and see the salvation of the Lord in this spiritual pregnancy that God has blessed you with!"

Are you struggling with letting go?

To allow God to take charge of any situation in your life is a wonderful experience; however, it can be hard to let go – actually release it to God so that you can experience His peace. Many of you, I'm sure, have the "take charge", the "I can do it myself"- the "my" attitude.

To have the revelation of the Peace of God is so sweet! You must trust and let it go. For as long as you keep holding on to your circumstance instead of trusting God to handle the situation, you will not be able to rest in the peace of God.

I recall a period in one of my spiritual pregnancies when the road seemed so... dark with a light somewhere far down the road. I believed that I was in the will of God, but at certain points in my spiritual pregnancy, I needed some assurance. One day, the Holy Spirit spoke to me, "I'm going to take care of you." It sounds like yesterday that I heard His voice, I remember it so vividly. That Word from the Holy Spirit is what I've rested on so many times throughout my different spiritual pregnancies – the different phases in my life. Regardless of how dark the road may seem, I've reminded myself, God told me, "I'm going to take care of you." Therefore, as long as I am in line with what He wants me to do, OBEDIENT, my God is going to keep His Word to me!

Even though I've had this Word from the Lord in conjunction with what His written Word promises me as I strive to obey the voice of the Lord and direction for my life, I have still been guilty of taking matters in my own hands at times. Each time that I've done this, I've felt no peace.

I recall one day becoming so fed up with my own actions; the "I've got this" attitude, until I had no choice but to totally let it go. So I physically went into a room where I was alone and shut the door. I then stood there as I cried out to God with tears running down my face, completely fed up to the point that I felt I was having a nervous breakdown (it is a shame that it has to go there sometimes). I had written down all of the situations in my life that "I" was trying to handle; folded the sheet of paper and put it in my hands, closed my eyes and put my hands together in an open cup position towards Heaven and envisioned myself walking towards God and handing Him the sheet of paper.

I remember crying to God saying, *"Daddy, right now I give these things to you. I am stepping out of the way; please handle it for me. I can't do it anymore. You said that You would take care of me. Daddy, I trust you to take over my life; let Your will be done from this day forth. I thank you Father for You are almighty, powerful, and great! Daddy, I love you. This I pray in the name of Jesus."* I then envisioned God folding His hands with my paper in it, then me moving away from Him, leaving it for Him to handle.

This was such an emotional moment for me. There's something about visualizing yourself putting it in God's hand and visualizing Him closing His hands around your situations as opposed to you just verbalizing it without the visual. Then telling yourself that if you continue to worry or think on the things that you've given to

God then you just as well consider that you've gone back to Him and snatched it out of His hands. At the same time saying to God, "Thanks, but no thanks, I've got this." Well, that's not a nice scene is it?

I would encourage you to have a similar personal ceremony regarding the situations that you are trying to handle in your life. When I finished my personal ceremony, I felt like a person letting go of a bad habit (and believe me, I know what that feels like). At the same time, I knew for sure that because I had given my heavy load to my "Daddy" and "I" let it go, He was going to handle it this time. I can't even describe the peace that came over me after this experience.

In summary, you can't have a successful spiritual birth without the peace of God (confidence, power, authority, rest) over you. The attacks from the enemy will come often and if you are not standing on a sure foundation, you will surely fall (Ephesians 6:15)! It is necessary to have peace about the direction and the call on your life, which can only come through the power of the Holy Spirit (Romans 14:17; Romans 15:13; Galatians 5:22)! Through the "Peace" of God (rest, confidence, power, authority) you will be able to stand the bumpy roads that you're sure to travel as you experience this transition in your life. Resting in God and His promises makes the bumps in the road a lot less noticeable. By letting go, you'll find peace. Otherwise, you'll continue to be restless if you try to hold on to what is out of your control. Let Go and let God! Trust me, "God's got this!"

Trust God and let it go so the peace of God can overtake you!

PEACE

Trust me and I'll give you Peace.
You're restless in this situation,
But it is me you don't see.
Your eyes are backwards,
And I'm forward.
Your focus is distorted because of
Your dilemma;
But, if you would trust me,
I'll bring you deliverance and
PEACE that passes all UNDERSTANDING!
(Proverbs 4:7)

The Code Language (Pray always in the Spirit)

Praying always with all prayer and supplication in the Spirit, and watching thereunto with all perseverance and supplications for all saints...(Ephesians 6:18)

This directive is so crucial in your spiritual pregnancy (e.g., spiritual battle). Remember, when you say "Yes" to what God has called you to do, the enemy will say "It is On!". Therefore, you must be prepared because the heat will turn up. In the spirit realm, the enemy can't understand anything you say when you pray in the Spirit. According to I Corinthians 14:2:

For he that speaketh in an unknown tongue speaketh not unto me, but unto God: for no man understands him; howbeit in the spirit he speaketh mysteries.

> Keep in mind, the enemy can only base his strategy off of what you speak and how you react.

Isn't that AWESOME?!

You are praying a mystery, ordering your team in the spirit realm to go at work in ways you would never know, building your spiritual ear, setting up defense against the attacks of the enemy, and strengthening your bond with God! The Bible says that we do not know how to pray as we ought, but the Spirit makes intercession for us (Romans 8:26). Also, when praying in the Spirit (the unknown tongue), you edify and improve yourself (I Corinthians 14:4).

When you're praying in the Spirit, the enemy doesn't know

how to set up his defense so quickly against you. I like to use a sports game as a prime example of how praying in the Spirit works as a defensive weapon in the spirit realm. When a coach notices the opposing team getting the upper hand or notices an opportunity that his team could take advantage of, the coach will call a time out. The team and the coach then get into a huddle while the coach quietly instructs the team on the next move, a proposed strategy towards victory (an offensive attack against the enemy) based on the current position of the game. Now, if the coach had a strategic offensive move and announced it over the microphone for the entire stadium to hear, that would not make much sense would it? Thereby, the necessity for the quiet huddle is so the opponent can not be prepared to set up defense against the strategy discussed quietly to the team. As the ole cliché goes… "Never let the right hand know what the left hand is doing."

Keep in mind, the enemy can only base his strategy off of what you speak and how you react. Although this being true, you should not keep quiet about the affirmations that God wants you to speak out regarding His promises or declarations that you must make, unless the Holy Spirit instructs you not to say anything aloud (He will do this sometimes). So, since the enemy can put things in your mind, but he can't read your mind, don't react on what the enemy puts there. If you're not sure that it is the enemy speaking to you or not, pray in the spirit immediately (you've already bound confusion, therefore, you don't have to pray that again. Just praise God for truth and pray in the spirit if a doubt should come to your mind). When you react, he plays on your emotions. The last thing you need to be is an emotional wreck in your spiritual pregnancy. So, watch what you say and PRAY ALWAYS IN THE SPIRIT!

You must realize, the enemy recognizes that you are pregnant in the Spirit. He knows that you've come with a purpose and his team has been strategizing for many years against the purposes of God's children. Truthfully, the enemy has had the upper hand for a while, without too much opposition from God's children. I'm not convinced that within the body of the children of God, the concept of the power derived as a result of praying in the Spirit or the process of being "guided" by the Spirit has been exercised. Otherwise, there would not be so much defeat and judgment amongst God's children. We must be sensitive to the Spirit, so that we can operate in and be completely guided by the Spirit, so that you can come through obstacles victoriously (Romans 8:5)! Just as food is for your flesh to stay strong, praying in the Spirit is food for your Spirit to stay strong.

This verse admonishes us to "Pray always in the Spirit". This doesn't mean just when you kneel down to pray and the prayer feels good to you so all of a sudden you began to pray in the Spirit. This is not just for prayer time. (Sometimes I think I pray more in the Spirit than I talk to people.) You should pray in the spirit as often as possible throughout the day. The war is going on all day, right? Well, you need to be constantly in the Spirit and praying in the Spirit as often as possible. Again, you are praying mysteries – setting up defense and instructing your spirit realm team. Let's not be clueless of the attacks of the enemy. We can't possibly know all of the attacks from the enemy. Hence, we have to pray in the spirit because again as the Word states, we don't know even how to pray.

*Likewise the Spirit also helpeth our infirmities: for we know not what we should pray for as we ought: but the Spirit Himself maketh intercession for us with groaning which "**cannot**" be uttered. (Romans 8:26)*

I'm reminded of another spiritual awakening while out of fellowship with God. Let's just say, the Spirit was willing, but my flesh was definitely weak (Matthew 26:41). My situation at the time was also not very safe. Anyhow, I remember cleaning up my studio loft and suddenly the Holy Spirit took control of me and I began to pray in the Spirit. I'm thinking to myself; "Where did that just come from?" It came over me so strong until I couldn't control it. I was actually nervous because I felt there was no way I could be praying in the Spirit with my lifestyle (this was prior to my revelation of righteousness). Some of you may feel that what I felt was true. Please remember that your flesh is never cleansed, only your Spirit (Galatians 5:17). Hence, you may go astray but the Spirit that lives within you is the Spirit of God, and He never changes regardless of how messed up you may see yourself! I am confident that God was intervening for my life in a way that I may never know at that moment He spoke through me in the Spirit. Thank God for the power of the Holy Spirit!

This is a powerful weapon in battle, especially as you are going through this spiritual pregnancy. This is a gift from God that is given to you with salvation. No, you do not have to "tarry" for the Holy Spirit and no, you do not have to be perfect to receive it. When you believe in God and accept that Jesus Christ died for the purpose of spiritual freedom, therefore making Him the leader of the Movement that we are all apart of, the gift of the Holy Spirit is yours. Just believe it and it's yours. You've got to stay in tune with your Commander-In-Chief, God, by hearing him clearly when He is directing you throughout this spiritual pregnancy. Praying in the Spirit is a vital key to that channel.

HAVE YOU RECEIVED THE GIFT OF THE HOLY SPIRIT?

According to the American Heritage College Dictionary, *gift* means *"something bestowed voluntarily and without compensation."* This means that the Holy Spirit is a gift from God to you, bestowed voluntarily and without compensation! Glory to God! Again, you don't have to put time in your walk of salvation before you receive the Holy Spirit.

This means, when you come to Him and He adopts you as His child, then He declares that you then have the power and the weapons needed to carry out the purpose that He has already planned for you. God is a God of completion – he doesn't half do anything. Hence, since he's aware of your position down here, He is going to make sure that His children are equipped from the moment they are conceived.

Before you pray, I want you to utilize your faith. Don't put your thinking into it; just allow God to speak through you. Believe in your heart and speak out of your mouth that when you complete this prayer or before, you'll have the evidence of the Holy Spirit with the evidence of speaking in tongues.

Pray this prayer:

> *Lord, according to your word I have been blessed with the*
> *Holy Spirit as a gift for accepting Jesus Christ as my Lord*

and Savior. I know that the Holy Spirit is my guide, my teacher that will show me all mysteries and teach me all things, and my friend according to John 14:26. Father, You said that I should always pray in the Spirit. Therefore, I know that it is Your will and desire that I receive the Holy Spirit with the evidence of speaking in tongues (Ephesians 6:15). So according to Your word I receive the gift that You've given me with the evidence of speaking in tongues. Right now, I believe by faith that when I open my mouth I will begin to speak as the Holy Spirit will give me utterance so that You may receive the Glory. In the name of Jesus I pray with thanksgiving (Ephesians 5:20; Colossians 3:17; Philippians 2:10). Now thank God for the evidence of the Holy Spirit by speaking in tongues!

> God speaks expressly here to state that again, without love, no matter what you do, how much faith you have… without love it means NOTHING!

Do not be discouraged and don't allow doubt, fear, and unbelief to deter you from the gift of God, the ability to do as you are admonished in Ephesians 6:15, which is to "pray always in the Spirit". Continue to believe and stand firm on your faith that you have received the gift of the Holy Spirit.

The Spiritual Voucher for the Maternity Clothes
(Check your love walk)

A new commandment I give unto you, that ye love one another; as I have loved you, that ye also love one another (John 13:34).

Walking in the love of God is very important if your spiritual armor is to work for you. Your armor works by faith and faith works by love (Galatians 5:6). Without love, your peace, your strength to stand and the Word of God will not have power when you speak it as you're going through a test if you don't have love! Remember, the armor works by Faith, which Faith works by Love!

The very acts of love, God demonstrated to us in the beginning through the sacrificing of Himself through His begotten Son, Jesus Christ for our sins. John 3:16 states, "For God so loved the world that He gave His only begotten son. That whosoever believeth in Him should not perish but have everlasting life." As children of God, we are commanded to love one another as He has loved us!

For scarcely for a righteous man will one die: yet peradventure for a good man some would even dare to die. But God commendeth His love toward us, in that, while we were yet sinners, Christ died for us." We were bound deep in sin, but God, in His infinite mercy and love for us, sent His only begotten Son to pay the price for "all" of our sins (Romans 5:7-8 – American Standard Version).

God gave up His begotten Son! This was an act of sacrifice, unselfishness, unconditional love. Are you sacrificing, unselfishly giving, and loving unconditionally? Or, are you thinking of all the good you've done, and how an individual deserves or doesn't deserve your love, your assistance, your tip, your time, your conversation, etc. This portion of the commandment is so crucial to the delivery of *True Purpose* in your life. You can not afford to not walk in LOVE!

Though I speak with tongues of men and of angels, and have not charity (love), I am become as sounding brass, or a tinkling cymbal. And though I have the gift of prophecy, and understand all mysteries, and all knowledge; and though I have all faith, so that could remove mountains, and have not charity, I am nothing." God speaks expressly here to state that again, without love, no matter what you do, how much faith you have, how much you go to church, if you are a Pastor, an Evangelist, how much you give, whatever good thing you think you may do, without love it means NOTHING (I Corinthians 13:1-2)!

Once I realized how God was requiring us to love, I then realized that it is humanly impossible to "love" how God wants us to "love" without being completely **guided** by the Holy Spirit so that the wisdom, knowledge and understanding that comes from the power of the Holy Spirit can over take your life as it did for Jesus (Luke 4:1; Luke 2:27; Luke 4:14). The American Heritage College Dictionary defines *love* as: "1. a tender feeling of affection and solicitude toward a person, such as that arising from kinship or a since of oneness. 2. A feeling of intense desire and attraction toward a person with whom one is disposed to make a pair; the emotion of sex or romance." The definition as defined in the American Heritage College Dictionary is very superficial (shallow) in comparison to this summary in the Holy Bible, I Corinthians 13:3-8:

Patient and kind
Not jealous or boastful
Not Arrogant or rude
Does not insist on its own way
Not irritable or resentful
Does not rejoice at wrong, but rejoices in the right
Bears all things, believes all things
Hopes all things, endures all things
Never ends or gives up

Wow!! God's love is supernatural. Consequently, this kind of love can not be accomplished unless through the power of the Holy Spirit.

The love of God is really the source of all of your power. If you are to be victorious in your life, you must walk in love. God is love and you are born of God, so you should act like your Father and love one another unconditionally (Luke 10:27). Jesus said that you are to even love the people that hate you and do for them expecting nothing in return and then, in I Corinthians 13:13, reminds you of this:

And now abideth faith, hope, charity, these three; but the greatest of these is charity." Even before a seed that you may have sown comes to fruition the way God intends for it to prosper in your life, you must walk in love (Luke 11:42).

Our Father says, "If ye love me, keep my commandments." (John 14:15). He also said that if you love Him, you would obey and serve Him with all your hearts, following His instructions (John 15:10). To follow God's instructions would be to establish His purpose in your life, which means that you will allow Him to completely control your life so that you can be fulfilled - blessed with true inner peace, joy, freedom, and love, without judgment or condemnation! All God wants to do is the exceptional, the abnormal, the out-the-box, the radical and to shine forth in your life as an expression of His love to you! No, you're not going to be perfect and God understands that you are a work in progress. However, God knows your heart and He knows if you are really trying to operate in His Agape love or not.

You're required to love "regardless" of your situation!

I'll give you an example of God's interpretation of love. Some years ago, I was in a relationship of abuse. It was the morning after an episode of abuse and about a few weeks after I had been seeking God for Agape love, I prepared breakfast as I usually would and I actually felt love all over me. It wasn't the kind of love that I was accustomed to: that silly, risky, compassionate, giddy kind of love, it was a love that I was unable to explain. It was as if I didn't remember the episode the night before for a moment and I said to the Lord, "What is this?" Without a thought, I've made breakfast and I'm not mad at him at all! He's going to think I'm stupid and that I accepted what He did to me."

My general habit was to always take him his meals after I prepared them for many years. However, the Holy Spirit spoke to me, "Prepare the meal and you don't have to take it to him; but let him know that it is down here." Then I suddenly felt a revelation come to me and I thought to myself, "There's a way I can act in love but stand strong at the same time. God will just give me wisdom on how to do it." So, I proceeded with my breakfast and I did as

God said to me. When I looked at him as he prepared his plate of food that I had made, I realized that I was not angry at him, but I felt sorry for him because of the spirit that was using him and he didn't even realize that he was being used! So, I told him, "I'm not mad at you, God will deal with you." He actually responded to me, "Don't say that to me."

I remember leaving the house and as I was driving to the freeway, I said to God, "This doesn't make since!" "He's going to think I'm a fool! I'm not angry at all with "him", just the spirit that used "him?!" Then, the Holy Spirit spoke to me, "Look at what Jesus went through." I spoke back to the Holy Spirit, "That's not fair; I'm not Jesus."

At that time I did not have the revelation that Jesus was here for-real in the "flesh" as you read in Chapter 3. Therefore, all of the ridicule and suffering that He endured yet continued to walk in love, not judgment I was required to do the same. In case you're wondering. Yes, I had gone to the police regarding the abuse that we were experiencing in my relationship but I didn't like the way they handled things. As a matter of fact, I felt that rather helped me and my children they caused our situation to be more dangerous. By the time this took place I knew that either I was going to get out on my own or, I was hoping that things would just get better. Although I realized that it was not the will of God for me or my children to be in that situation, while I was there it was my requirement as a child of God to "Walk in Love" just as Jesus did with his offenders.

NOTE: I am not advising that you do not stand up for yourself in a situation of abuse for those that are in a situation of abuse. I am, however, stating that you need ***God's Love*** and ***God's Wisdom*** for many of you to be delivered out of that situation of abuse that you may be in. At the end of the day, I learned that Love breaks all shackles and my children and I were soon delivered from that situation with the wisdom that God continued to give me.

CHAPTER 6

Common Spiritual Pregnancy Symptoms

(e.g., pregnancy symptoms)

- ## The Bad Symptoms

Reference:

Bad symptom —————————→Infection—————→Spirit to bind

Cure from bad symptom———→ Antibiotic————→Spirit to loose

Prayer —————————————→Instructions to take antibiotics

- ## The Good Symptoms

Common Spiritual Pregnancy Symptoms

(e.g., pregnancy symptoms)

"Now that you're dressed for this spiritual pregnancy, gain understanding of the symptoms you may have in this process. Some are good and some are bad. As for the bad, gain knowledge of how to successfully overcome the obstacles you may face as you climb the ladder to ultimate fulfillment in your life."

Throughout your spiritual pregnancy (your transition – your spiritual warfare), you will be faced with many attacks from the enemy (your opponent). If you are not aware of how to fight your opponent, you will most likely abort the spiritual birthing process due to the lack of understanding and awareness. To prevent spiritual abortion, you need to know how to ward off common attacks from the enemy in the spirit realm. In addition, you need to understand how to discern if what you're experiencing is a result of God altering things in your life, or if it is the enemy attacking you. You need to know when to battle and when to ride the course. Similar to natural pregnancy for women, all symptoms are not bad, but the doctor generally makes the woman aware of all known symptoms so that she may understand how to get relief from, or how to prevent the symptoms that are occurring.

In a natural pregnancy, women can try a remedy or take a peel to subside sickness. In the spirit realm everything you experience is intangible. In this battle you are required to counteract the symptoms in the spirit realm with the weapons and authority that God gives us in the Word of God, just as Jesus did in Matthew 4:3-11 (Chapter 3). Keep in mind, Jesus was consistent with the Word of God and He was full of the Holy Spirit, so His jabs with the Sword (the Word of God) were powerful and effective (Matthew 4:10-11; Acts 10:38; John 2:22).

It is important to know what to bind and loose and how to bind and loose in the spirit realm so that your Sword is utilized effectively. You have to take authority over your own life. Wake up and put off the works of darkness (Romans 13:12-14). You need to understand the root cause of the infection that may be present in your life, so that you may terminate the infection (issue) from your life forever!

I'll use a tree as an example: A tree has roots, branches and leaves. What happens if you cut a branch off of a tree? Generally, the branch will grow back and often times that one branch will produce more leaves than before. Likewise in the spirit realm, you must kill a spirit from the root with the power and authority that God has given you so that it will not continuously present itself in your life. Eventually taking over and robbing you of God's promises – your life's fulfillment.

This process of spiritual pregnancy will not be all peaches and cream. Some spiritual pregnancies will be less challenging than others and vice-versa. Not every symptom will be applicable to every person or specific spiritual pregnancy. However, you have to stay on top of your game, recognizing all of the subtle points as well as the obvious points. It is necessary to study the opponent so that you may be skilled against any attack!

If you know the root of a spirit, you can go straight to the root, calling it out by name, and ultimately killing the entire evil tree. To simplify, there are several symptoms that come with a "cold" (e.g. sneezing, coughing, body chills, runny nose, stuffy nose, runny eyes). If you begin to cough and sneeze, typically, you will be considered to be infected with a cold.

You don't have to see all of the symptoms that come with a cold, to treat yourself for all of the cold symptoms. There are several types of cold medicines available; however, I'm sure if you have any signs of a cold, your option would be the cold medicine that gets rid of all of the symptoms. Otherwise, you chance taking the medicine just for the cough and the sneezing and then later having to go back within a week or so for the medicine that will rid you of all symptoms.

The same scenario applies in the spirit realm.. It is not necessary to have evidence of all the spirits on the evil tree, for all of the spirits to be present within you. Generally, the enemy will attack you in a very subtle way (the branches or the leaves) so that you do not recognize the big picture (the entire evil tree). Another example, if you were battling with alcoholism and then you stopped drinking as much, you may believe that you were completely free from any addiction that may try to take hold of you in the future, especially the alcoholism that you've recently overcome. For you to not recognize "addiction" as the spirit it is, makes you very vulnerable to other addictions, including resorting back to alcoholism.

The spirit of "addiction", which is a "branch" on the spiritual evil tree of Bondage, produces many leaves. Addiction alone may include over eating, smoking, shopping, coffee, too much TV, etc.

Therefore, it is crucial that you understand what you're dealing with so the enemy does not play your ignorant card. Honestly, that's how the enemy has been able to challenge you, your family, or your friends in the way that he has. Remember, for the lack of knowledge men have perished (I Corinthians 15:34).

Once you recognize the existence of a spirit in your life, it is necessary to take charge of the spirit and denounce it from your life. (If you're having difficulty understanding what I'm speaking of, ask the Lord to give you revelation and declare the Spirit of God and His understanding within you now according to John 14:26). When my children were little I received the revelation of the spirit realm. Even then it really made a lot of since to me. So to ensure that my children were not subjected to some of the things that my family and their father's family had been subjected to, I wanted to educate them. I asked the Lord for wisdom on how to educate my children about Spiritual Warfare and He did.

I set my children down one day at the table and I explained to them about Spiritual Warfare and how the Lord said that we wrestle not against flesh and blood, but against principalities and the rulers of darkness (Ephesians 6:13). I then began to share with them on a level they could understand, how things work in the spirit realm and that we were going to take charge over the enemy with the authority that God gave us in Matthew 16:19. I'll share this with you because I want you to have the knowledge of how the spirit realm works so that you can be more than a conquer (Romans 8:37).

I told my children, "Evil spirits are like squatters in your house. If you had a squatter in your basement and you didn't know that he was there, he could stay there for years learning everything about you. Learning when you come, when you go, what makes you angry, what makes you happy, and so on and on. After a while, the squatter may even feel as though your house is just as much his house as it is yours. Now once you recognize the squatter, you'd obviously tell him to leave, immediately. You may even ask, "How did you even get in here?! At this moment, because it is your house and in your house you have authority, the squatter realizes that he must leave immediately. This is not to say that the squatter left without a fight. Nonetheless, if the squatter puts up too much of a fight, you have the right to kill him because he is trespassing on your property."

My children were so cute. Their eyes got bigger and bigger, and I said to them, "The enemy has been squatting in your house (your mind, your life), and we've got to get the enemy and his entourage out today!" They were excited and they both said, "Yeah!" I explained to them how we were going to take charge of these squatters and that I would share with them every spirit that I could think of that ran in my family's and their father's family's blood line. You should have seen their eyes when they saw all of the familiar spirits that ran in their blood-line. My son said, "Mommy, all of that is in me?" I said, "It's all in your blood-line sweetie, so there are more than likely squatters in your house. However, you're going to call them out by name from the root and put them out of your house today! The buck stops here!" I then had my children repeat after me as we took the list of familiar spirits (the common traits within our family) that I knew of and we began to bind every evil spirit on our list out of our lives from the roots. This was a laboring exercise, but very fulfilling! For those of you who do not know of your family, ask the Lord to reveal to you what's in your blood-line that should be bound out of your life. Ask God to show you the most secret parts of you (Acts 15:8; I John 3:20).

Something that is very crucial for you to understand as well is the authority that you have in your "house" (your mind, your life) verses someone else. For example, I may have knowledge of spiritual warfare and my children may be my children; however, I don't have the authority over their house (their minds; their lives) that they do. I can cause some chaos by praying against the spirits that I know may be present, but at the end of the day, my children can invite or allow to stay in their house whomever or whatever they wish, rather knowingly or unknowingly.

I'm sure some of you reared your children one way and some of your children turned out to be completely opposite of how you reared them. You may think, "What happened to the 'Train up a child in a way that he should go, and when he is old he will not depart (Proverbs 22:6)?'" Some of you may wonder how your

> Some of you may wonder how your children ended up down the same path you tried to shield them from.

children ended up down the same path you tried to shield them from. For example, you may have kept your child from being around certain people and out of a particular environment with the intent of shielding your child from bad behavioral patterns. You may have also done everything within your power to prevent yourself from going down the same path that maybe your mother or father went down, or, even an aunt or uncle, yet you found yourself doing the same thing you swore you would never do. On the other hand, some of you bypassed the cycles, but regardless of your efforts of training your children in the way you wanted them to go in life, you have found evidence of what "you" conquered and maybe even your children conquered, within the lives of your grandchildren. Sadly enough, the majority of you don't understand how to gain total victory over any particular area in your life or how to break the cycle.

You must consider that you may have had strength to do what was necessary to prevent that spirit from taking control in your life, but the same spirit will continue to lurch in your family until it finds a resting place. Resting in someone that does not have the strength to resist (I Peter 5:8). Thus, the reason for the knowledge of spiritual warfare: "It AIN'T no joke!" as I radically state often times. You either gain knowledge of it, or it can take control of your life and your families' life for generations!

In the spirit realm, if you bind up the spirit from the root, you then bind up all spirits that come on that evil spiritual tree, the branches the branches and the leaves. Without the understanding of what you're binding and loosing, you will find yourself in a world-wind, constantly battling the same thing over and over again throughout your life.

Just as we are to leave an inheritance for our children in the natural, we are to leave them a spiritual inheritance. The knowledge of "Spiritual Warfare" is truly an eternal blessing, leaving them the keys to TOTAL VICTORY and the tools of overcoming great obstacles in their lives for an eternity!

In this chapter you gain understanding on the most common spiritual pregnancy symptoms: good and evil. With regards to the evil, I will address how to become victorious over the attack of the enemy so that you may successfully birth what God has planted in you. You'll also read about the good symptoms that will occur during your spiritual pregnancy and how to enjoy this entire process even through what seems to be the down times.

Common Spiritual Pregnancy Symptoms (Bad): The following are the roots of the Evil Spiritual Trees addressed in this Chapter: Seducing Spirits, Lying Spirit, Whoredom, Haughtiness, and Slothfulness.

Common Spiritual Pregnancy Symptoms (Good): The following are great Spirits from God's Good Spiritual Tree addressed in this Chapter: Joy, Perseverance, Strong Faith, Confidence, Courage, Humble Nature, Peace, and Love.

The Bad Symptoms

SPIRIT OF FEAR (e.g., an infection)

For God has not given us the spirit of fear; but of power, and of love, and of a sound mind. (II Timothy 1:7)

The branches on the tree of the Spirit of Fear:

1. **Fears, Phobias**: Proverbs 10:24; 2 Timothy 1:7
2. **Nightmares**: Psalm 91:5-6; Isaiah 54:14
3. **Torment, Horror**: 1 John 4:18
4. **Heart Attacks**: Psalm 55:4; Luke 21:26-28; John 14:1, 27
5. **Fear of Man**: Proverbs 29:25; Jeremiah 1:8, 17-19; Ezekiel 2:6-7; 3:9
6. **Fear of Death**: Psalm 55:4; Hebrews 2:14-15
7. **Anxiety, Stress**: I Peter 5:7
8. **Lack of Trust, Doubt**: Matthew 8:26

When is the Spirit of Fear most likely to present itself during your spiritual pregnancy? Fear may present itself at anytime there appears to be an open door. In addition to Fear itself, pay close attention to Lack of Trust, Doubt and Anxiety as specified below:

1. **Fear**: Conception and 1st period
2. **Lack of Trust, Doubt and Anxiety**: Periods of Delivery, Labor and After-Birth

NOTE: Although there are periods specified, understand that you may have evidence of these spirits (symptoms) at anytime during your spiritual pregnancy. Listed for your reference are the periods in which they are most commonly noticed. It may vary from pregnancy to pregnancy and person to person.

Fear: Conception and 1st Period

The American Heritage College Dictionary defines fear as: "1. A feeling of agitation and anxiety caused by present or imminent danger. 2. A feeling of disquiet or apprehension: a fear of looking foolish." According to II Timothy 1:7, God has not given you the spirit of fear. Know that, through God, who is almighty, powerful, and truth you have nothing to fear! I'm sure many of you can appreciate the interpretation of fear in the second definition, "a fear of looking foolish." In the period of Conception you may feel forced to make decisions that may cause you to appear as though you're crazy to many; however, you must continue to stand strong. Remember, God has already forewarned us that what we do in the spirit realm as we are guided by the Holy Spirit "will", not "may", look foolish to men who are not operating in the Spirit (I Corinthians 2:14). Hence, do not allow fear of what people may think of you with regards to the decisions that you must make to follow the call of God on your life, deter you from moving on to or continuing the process of your spiritual pregnancy. Again, "It is not about you! It is about God!"

In the 1st Period, you are going through the pruning stage and it can get a bit rough for many people. In this period, I've known people to feel as though they were going to die of depression, or felt their world was crumbling before them. Thus, it is very important to have knowledge of this spiritual pregnancy process so that you do not act out of fear of your circumstance, which could ultimately result in a spiritual abortion due to poor judgment or discernment. Know your position in God and who He is to you – Truth and

Power! Know that whatever is getting ready to happen is in divine order because you are willing to do as God has planned for you – willing to live a life of fulfillment.

I know that it can get a bit scary for many, but let go and let God. Something to think about: One day when I was counseling someone, the Holy Spirit gave me a visual of a person hanging on the side of a building with their bare hands. It came to me, God sees that many of you attempt to do this, not trusting that if you let go, wherever you land and at whatever level, his parachute will always go up with perfect timing if you seek His plan for your life. Although you may perceive yourself as falling or everything around you as crumbling down, you will land at whatever level He has planned for you safe and sound and without damage. Just let go and have no fear. God's got your back. Think of Superman, not Hancock.

Doubt and Unbelief:
Periods of Delivery, Labor, and After-Birth

> This feeling of anxiety (e.g., apprehension, fear, and agitated desire) is very common in the spiritual pregnancy process...

In the natural birthing experience, many women experience anxiety as they draw closer to delivery. This feeling of anxiety (e.g., apprehension, fear, and agitated desire) is very common in the spiritual pregnancy process as well. By this time you are more than ready to get this process over. Although it is an intangible experience, by this period, you can see yourself right where God wants you to be, so you just want to deliver - TODAY! However, you must be careful to stay in God's timing and to have patience (Luke 8:15). Everything is in divine order!

At times, in the Periods of Spiritual Labor and Delivery, it is very likely that you may question, "Did I do the will of God?" "Did I take the wrong turn?" "Maybe I didn't hear God correctly regarding my *True Purpose*?" Even after everything that you would have been through during your entire spiritual pregnancy and the confirmations from God throughout the process of your spiritual pregnancy, the enemy will come to attack your faith, which will more than likely cause you to doubt everything that you have believed God for in this process. Don't be dismayed but stand firm on God's promise to you and know that God is All Power and He is not a God that He should lie. His word will not return to Him void of power (Isaiah 55:11)

I must emphasize that even in the period of After-Birth the spirit of Doubt will generally present itself very strong in an effort to make you doubt the delivery that God has just birthed through you. An example of a few doubts that may cross your mind, "I can't move forward with this project, my life is a wreck, so how could I be an example." Someone else may think, "God is perfect, so with the flaws in this, it can't be from God." Many things may run through your mind; however, you are judging from the natural eye, but what God has birthed through you, is perfect in the eyes of God and the message that God intends for you and others to receive will be received as God intended from the moment He chose you to conceive the gift. He knew your flaws when He chose you for that particular purpose, but what He's done through you is perfect.

In summary, do not allow fear to cripple you from enjoying or moving forward to complete manifestation of your gift. Release what God has given you and watch the manifestation of good fruit come back to you and to many others as a result of your obedience! The enemy attacks you with the Spirit of Fear so that you can back down and for God to not get the Glory in your life, which will ultimately be the salvation of many upon the earth.

Fear of Death:
Period of Delivery and Labor

I feel led to touch on this subject. In the natural, Jesus experienced a physical death, which was a part of His *True Purpose*. The enemy overwhelmed Him with fear as He neared the completion of His purpose here on earth as read in Chapter 3. Jesus was so overwhelmed with fear until He asked God if He could lift the cup from Him (Mark 14:36). Today, one may say as you near the birthing of your gift, "'Lord, can we go another route?' 'Do I have to do this?' or, 'Lord, please answer me, please, I feel so lost!'"

Although Jesus was very aware of His death, I'm sure just like you and I, He did not know exactly the detail of His journey down the road until He reached that road. Sure, He knew that He would be crucified, but did He realize how unmercifully He would be beaten in its explicit detail? I believe that He did not. Not that He couldn't of known, but just like everything else in this process, God informs you as you need to be informed and in His timing. What would be the point of God showing Him the anguish, the lashes, the evil in its explicit nature? It was enough to just understand that He was facing death. This is why the enemy uses the opportunity to overwhelm you with fear at this crossroad, just like the enemy did to Jesus in attempts of preventing Jesus from moving forward.

Although at this crossroad, many will experience great feelings of fear, there is one truth in which you should remain confident, and this truth will be your strength – there is great victory and fulfillment and to God will be all of the glory! Another truth is when you've endured spiritual pregnancy to the point of Delivery and Labor, you are committed to complete and implement the *True Purpose* that God has called for you. By now, I'm sure you realize that when you said "Yes" to this process you committed to die to self. On the other hand, you must also realize that for this spiritual pregnancy, regardless of what you are going to face, even if it means a natural death, you are to stay the course and not spiritually abort the gift. Finally, understand that your fulfillment is for you as well as others so always keep in mind the big picture.

In the last period, the enemy will try many in this area of fear, in conjunction with fear as it relates to doubt and unbelief. This is very similar to natural pregnancy. In the natural, when a woman delivers her baby, she is having a near death experience. It is a very painful but considered to be a rewarding experience (challenges, pain and all) once that bundle of joy is birthed into the world.

In the spirit realm, the enemy may attack you with this fear of death to the point you may feel as though it is going to happen in the natural. For many people, the only death you will experience is the death of the life you once knew – a glorious transition. You're making a complete turn around in your life – graduating from one level to the next and the enemy hates it! On the other hand, there are some people that may experience death in the natural and God will give you peace about your destiny. Although it is true that if we all live long enough here on earth we will all die one day, death may be a part of someone's purpose at an earlier point in life. If this is so, God has already prepared you for that and it will not take place until God's plan for you is complete here on earth if you are following His plan. I don't care if there has been a threat on your life in the natural, as long as you are in obedience with the plan for your life, your *True Purpose*, God's perfect plan for you, "No weapon formed against you shall prosper!" Regardless, the spirit of fear should not be allowed to cloud your view from God's plan for your life. Stay the course and remember: the joy of the Lord is your strength (Nehemiah 8:10)! If you are God's child, death is beautiful and it is nothing to fear! Just continue the path that God has planned for you.

> *Take Notice! I tell you a mystery (a secret truth, an event decreed by the hidden purpose or counsel of God). We shall not all fall asleep [in death], but we shall all be changed (transformed)* (I Corinthians 15:50)

How to destroy the Spirit of Fear and every branch on its tree:

According to Matthew 16:19:

> *Verily, I say unto you, whatsoever ye shall bind on earth shall be bound in heaven: and whatsoever ye shall loose on earth shall be loosed in heaven.*

Bind: Spirit of Fear (e.g., an infection)

Loose: Love, Power, and a Sound Mind (e.g., the antibiotic)

The warfare prayer:
(e.g., the instructions on taking the antibiotic)

According to Matthew 16:19, I bind up the Spirit of Fear and every spirit that comes with the Spirit of Fear: Fears, Phobias, Nightmares, Night Terrors, Torment, Horror, Heart Attacks, Fear of Man, Fear of Death, Anxiety, Stress, Lack of Trust, Doubt. Spirit of Fear, I bind you up from the root, according to the authority that God has given me in His word and I loose according to II Timothy 1:7, the Spirit of Love, Power, and a Sound Mind! I cast you into the abyss - never to return! You are not welcomed in my life - my temple! No weapon formed against me shall prosper as God assures me in (Isaiah 54:17)! No Weapon! This I pray in the Name of Jesus!

NOTE: It is also great to pray in the spirit at this point.

Now begin to worship our Father, for He is Almighty and worthy to be praised. Praise Him for the Victory! Praise God that you have Love, Power, and a Sound Mind! Praise Him for His promised Word, in which He says that His word will not return unto Him void (Isaiah 55:11)!

SPIRIT OF SEDUCING SPIRITS
(e.g., an infection)

Now the Spirit speaketh expressly, that in the latter times
some shall depart from the faith giving heed to seducing
spirits, and doctrines of devils. (II Timothy 4:1)

The branches on the spiritual tree of the Spirit of Seducing Spirits:

1. **Hypocritical Lies**: I Timothy 4:1; Proverbs 12:22
2. **Deception, Liar (e.g., white lies)**: 1 John 2:23-28;
   2 Timothy 3:13; 2 Thessalonians 2:10
3. **Attraction to False Prophets, Magic, etc.**:
   Acts 8:7-19; Mark 13:22
4. **Lusts and passions of the flesh:** James 1:13-16
5. **Seducers, Enticers:** Job 36:18; Proverbs 1:10;
   Proverbs 16:29; Matthew 18:6; James 1:14
6. **Lured by evil (ways, objects or people):**
   Proverbs 12:26; Acts 3:26

When is the Spirit of Seducing Spirits most likely to present itself during your spiritual pregnancy? Seducing Spirits may present itself at anytime there appears to be an open door. Pay close attention to the entire spiritual tree.

1. **The Entire Spiritual Tree:** The entire spiritual pregnancy

NOTE: Listed for your reference are the periods in which there most commonly noticed. It may vary from pregnancy to pregnancy and person to person.

*In the last days perilous times shall come. For men shall be lovers of their own selves, covetous, boasters, proud, blasphemers, disobedient to parents, unthankful, unholy, without natural affection, trucebreakers, false accusers, incontinent, fierce, despisers of those that are good, traitors, heady, high-minded, lovers of pleasures more than lovers of God; having a form of godliness, but denying the power thereof: from such turn away...But evil men and **SEDUCERS shall wax worse and worse, deceiving, and being deceived*** (I Timothy 4:1; 2 Timothy 3:1-5; 13-15) .

This spirit is so... prevalent today amongst the earth! You must be careful! People, be careful and do not be deceived!

According to Matthew 4:3-11; Jesus was led to the wilderness by the "Holy Spirit" to be tempted by the enemy. I need you to not overlook that according to the Word of God, prior to this temptation, Jesus had consecrated for 40 days and 40 nights. He had abided in the Lord for 40 days and 40 nights through fasting and praying. You may not have to fast 40 days and 40 nights to establish or maintain a life of consecration; however, you do have to maintain consistency in your worship, your time with God and your time in the Word of God – continuously abiding in God (I John 2:27-28).

After the consecration and time that Jesus had abided with God, He was full of the Holy Spirit; thereby, I'm sure, more sensitive to the voice of the Holy Spirit. However, the enemy came to Jesus with temptation of what Jesus already knew He was and was capable of through the authority of God (Matthew 4:3, 5-6, 8-9; Luke 4:1). To discern that it was the enemy, Jesus had to be full of the Holy Spirit. Jesus already knew who He was in God; the authority, the power. He already knew that He could speak whatever and it would be so. So, do you notice that the enemy did not tempt Jesus with something that was not true and out of the realm of possibilities for

Jesus through God. This Seducing Spirit also tempted Jesus with the Word of God (Matthew 4:6). Jesus, however, knew that this was not the voice of the Lord, but it was the voice of the enemy! How do you think Jesus knew this? He was consecrated; thereby, prepared for such an attack from the enemy!

I love how God sent Jesus here on earth to live through this example. Some may say, "Jesus was NEVER seduced by the enemy!" You're right, Satan didn't succeed in his attempt to seduce; however, Satan definitely tried (Matthew 4:3-11). OK, you can hold your seat, because I strongly suggest, the ONLY reason Jesus was not seduced was due to Him being full of the Holy Spirit at that time (Matthew 4:2). This is how He was able to discern the voice of the Lord. I know, some of you may wonder "How could she imply that it was even possible for 'Jesus' to be seduced?" You may think that it **never** could have happened to Him. In fact, you are wrong. Without repeating Chapter 3 on the subject of Jesus, I'll remind you, Jesus was here in the **flesh** like you and I, with the possibility to sin, like you and I (I John 4:2; I John 4:3).

Jesus was here for a purpose; as an example and to die for our sins so that we may live a righteous life as a result of His sacrifice, obtaining right relationship with God through Him (Matthew 16:20-23; Matthew 5:21). The choices that He made of obedience, sacrifice, consecration, and love affected His outcome. Again, God gave us this example because He wanted us to follow suit after Jesus; His choices, His lifestyle. For you to be capable of discerning a Seducing Spirit, you will need to be abiding in the Holy Spirit. I can't stress this point enough, don't get it twisted, you must abide in the Lord so that you can be prepared for the enemies' attack

- the "seducing spirit" that Satan will present to confuse you in your mind or in the physical. Beware! Everybody that is speaking the Word of God is not of God! You may even be presented with what you know God has promised you. Yet, you must seek the Holy Spirit for assurance that it is Him speaking or presenting an offer to you. You must be careful that you do not fall prey to a Seducing Spirit (I Timothy 4:1)! However, if you are not consecrated, you are very likely to fall prey!

3 ways to establish a more sensitive spirit to the Holy Spirit (the voice of God):

- Pray always in the Spirit
  (This is a crucial key on the battlefield.)
- Spend time in the Word of God daily
- Spend time talking to God (the Holy Spirit) daily

I was seduced by a "Seducing Spirit"

It is horrible that I did not recognize this spirit – I thought it was God blessing me as He promised, "Glory to God!" I exclaimed when it presented itself as a light. However, I could not recognize the darkness in this spirit. At that time, I knew that God was getting ready to elevate me to another level. I could feel the transition taking place; however, I realize now that where God was sending me was quit the contrary of where I was really headed. I needed more money to go in the direction that I thought God was sending me. Eventually, I realized doors opening up in ways they had not before and I continued to give God all the Glory for everything. There was no one that could deter me from the mission that God had placed on my life. I also know that the enemy was plotting against my purpose. I can only imagine what's going on in the Spirit realm.

Well, in my office one day as I'm overseeing the view of downtown Detroit from the office that I knew God placed me in, I cry out to God, "Lord, you've placed me here and I know from this place you will send me the financial victory that needs to take place in my life so that I can continue towards the purpose for my life." "Lord, you know what I need." You said that faith without works is dead, so, I'm standing and believing on your word for this promise as I work daily."

It didn't take long after that prayer that someone was referred to me that seemed to have every connection and answer to everything that I had been standing on for years. I was connected with the "Chief" of the company and his partner that could make everything happen. I had been researching the process of buying corporations and this "Chief" had all of the resources that would enable me to purchase the corporations at a much cheaper price than I had ever anticipated. My intention was to position the new corporation as a subsidiary to my current corporation for the purposes of increasing my company's portfolio.

"What could be wrong with this?" The chiefs were "God fearing" individuals and in my eyes they were to be commended for their success. I was proud of them and felt that I was embarking upon a great strategic business relationship and entering the life that God had promised via this encounter and the proposed investment.

Well, they wined and dined me for about 2 months, nothing out of the norm for CEOs building a strategic relationship. After the resources and the references which included a Bank Manager, all checked favorably along with a few successful transactions, I felt comfortable to move forward with my purchase of the corporations that would be structured by the company that I had been dealing with. The company that I thought was sent by God. There was nothing that anyone could tell me to make me believe that this was not legitimate and that it was not the will of God. I was excited about the transactions and was just anticipating my company being put in a better position financially to receive the "inheritance" that the Lord had promised.

Were there red flags, now that I think back? Why – Yes! However, they were blind to me at the time as a result of the lack of consecration in my life, I am led to believe! I praised God, glorified God, and shouted to the masses that my promise had come through and as a result, the world was going to be transformed! Yes, I gave all of the Glory to God, but I was too blind to see the trick of the enemy. However, the way this transaction would be done would have been acceptable in man's eyes, but it was not acceptable in God's eyes. I was going to buy the "paper" of this corporation without the responsibility of function. I felt that must be the way to do what needed to be done to get the result that I needed per my then knowledge obtained from several sources. After all, the last thing I wanted was the responsibility of another company on my hands. Buying the "paper" was just fine with me.

This was not God, obviously. However, many people do similar transactions and it works out just fine. In my case, there was even an attorney and an accountant involved. Hey, it must be

> God doesn't need the enemy's deceptive tactics to help you get ahead.

legitimate, right? Not! God doesn't need the enemy's deceptive tactics to help you get ahead. The Lord told me, "Sweetheart, there is a right way and a righteous way". "I am calling for a holy people and a separate people. I need you to come from amongst the world and be ye separate. Do it my way. I will take care of you and the blessing will be eternal." Needless to say, the company was fraud and I lost a ton of money, including other investors who were investing in this corporate purchase.

At the time, I thought that I was in the will of God. I wasn't going to do anything but "bless the world" and my investors would obtain their financial goals. So I cried to God, "Lord, why did this happen to me? I didn't here you telling me no. Why Lord, Why! Why!" Once I began to pray to God, the majority of what I had worked for was gone into this investment, I wanted to be as Lot's wife and continue to look back, condemning myself (even now it hurts in the pit of my stomach – How could I be so blind? NOT ME... I don't make mistakes like that). But God! But God! How could I tell you or began to help you understand (don't worry, I'm not saying that it was God that did this to me; however, I am saying that it was God that allowed this to happen to me for a reason and He took this situation and worked it out for His good in spite of the devils tactics to tear me completely down). I've never been defrauded or seduced in this manner – never in the life of my career!

Just as the Lord warned us in His word of the last day, "...Seducers shall wax worse and worse, deceiving..." (II Timothy 3:1-5; 13-15). Through association, I accompanied these people at their outings, "elite bars" and restaurants, etc. I thought to myself, "After all, I've worked hard so it's OK to have a good time." Bottom-line, I was not consecrated!! I was in error and under a spirit of deception! Everyone that confesses Christ is not Christ-like and is not assumed to be trusted. I put trust in man and it back-fired. I did not consult the Holy Spirit, but I assumed based on my research. Consequently, I fail prey to the Seducing Spirit.

I was warned...

Wow, I remember speaking with a client just a few years prior to this occurrence. I presented to this client an opportunity to receive a line of credit so that she could leverage money to buy some great real estate deals. To receive this line of credit she would have to go "stated" (this means that your income is stated and you don't have to show on paper what you make, which is the purpose of a stated transaction). This is a format that was widely used in the mortgage industry and is a major reason the market is the way it is today (too many people being financed for properties that were well out of their range of affordability). There was nothing unlawful about this transaction. It is simply a creative way of completing a transaction when a client can't show on paper enough income but has an approved score. Well, she had a great score and was going to buy solid real estate deals that would definitely put her and the bank in a winning position. She'd buy the properties using the banks money for properties 30 cents on the dollar and then she'd refinance, using a small portion of the equity to buy another property that she would

> The Lord told me, "Sweetheart, there is a right way and a righteous way". "I am calling for a holy people and a separate people."

deal…thereby, putting her in the position to pay the bank back their money and holding on to a property with substantial equity. Well, what could be wrong with that?

She says to me, "I'll think about it." I'm thinking, "You're crazy, what part of what I just said did you not understand?" You're here now with no money, you want to get into Real Estate investing, I'm giving you cream of the crop properties and I'm going to educate you in the process. What is there to lose? What? I'm thinking, "A blind man could see this is a chance of a life-time".

She leaves that day and calls my Secretary to schedule another appointment with me. I'm thinking, "They always come back. Poor thing, she was just nervous, after all she had been mistreated by other people in the industry that did not know what they were doing. So, I understand her dilemma."

To my surprise, she comes to the office for her second appointment. As she's sitting across from me, I think to myself, "Great, let's get this ball rolling." I'm excited for this opportunity that this young lady is getting ready to embark upon. So I'm thinking, she's young and she's got a great future ahead of her (I wish I had someone to coach and develop me when I was her age). Well, as I'm waiting to hear what she has to say, she crosses her legs and says to me, "I thought about everything we talked about before. Although I want to get started and I feel that you can really help me, this is a lie. God will not bless a lie. If I have to lie to get the line of credit, I don't want it." I'm thinking, "She's crazy – really, she's crazy!"

She continues, "And God is not going to bless you how He wants to bless you as long as you are a part of a lie." I then explain to her, "Sweetheart, this is just a stated deal that is lawful and people do it all the time." "You're not really lying, you're stating the income and it's not too far off of the reality of your income; consider it as calling those things that are not as though they are." "If I thought that you couldn't pay back the loan, I wouldn't care what credit you had, I wouldn't do it. I've turned many people away who I knew couldn't afford it and I had no parts of it. Besides, Lenders come in my office and talk about individuals that do stated deals and don't state enough income to make it fly." I wasn't trying to deceive her, I was speaking with my business hat and what I thought was "really" right. In my book it was just the procedure.

You must understand, there are a lot of deals and transactions that are lawful to man, but may place you as a child of God in a compromising position. There's a right way and there's a righteous way. According to the Holy Bible, there is a way that seems right unto a man, but the end will lead to destruction (Proverbs 14:12). (Hello! Can we pause and take a look at the market – the economy?)" OK, back to the point…

As I look back on that day she was in my office, I'll never forget her words and her concept, which was God's concept. Yeah, she would have gotten a deal and she would have made money and the bank would have been paid back shortly after the transaction, but she would have compromised her position spiritually and for nothing, I mean nothing, would she do that. God bless her, in the Name of Jesus! But, how much greater will God and has God blessed her as a result of her commitment to the TRUTH? She was consecrated and was not able to be deceived by the spirit that was deceiving me into believing that I was justified by the law of man. I wasn't! The world isn't! Lying is lying however you look at it! By adopting the spirit of lying in your life you adopt Seducing Spirits that can all rob you of what God has promised you. Don't think that the enemy is not working overtime to prevent you from the blessings of God, from you going forth with your spiritual pregnancy and successfully implementing *True Purpose* in your life! This is the last and evil day and God WILL WIN this battle. Let's just say, "You either get in line or get off the pot". God is not going to be short-changed! So, you either do it His way or you will not be eternally blessed. Yes, God loves everyone but your decisions determine your quality of life, your fulfillment, peace, happiness, and joy – your Total Victory in life! What quality of life do you want and do you want for your children? Your decisions not only determine destiny for you, but it also determines the destiny and challenges that will be presented to your children. Remember: Life is a revolving door.

Another point that I must make: I've known Pastors that are "on fire for God", and members of the church that abide by the same concept I once did. "If it is alright by law, it is alright by me." It may be easy for you to get sucked into the world's way and it seems harder for you to remove yourself from the world's way because that's all you know (Romans 12:2). Recognize that God has called you separate from the worlds way (John 17:16; Acts 24:16; Luke 21:34). According to the Word of God, the Seducing Spirit will get worse and worse in the last days (I Timothy 4:1). Therefore, you must stand on guard at all times.

How to destroy Seducing Spirits and every branch on its tree:

According to Matthew 16:19:

Verily, I say unto you, whatsoever ye shall bind on earth shall be bound in heaven and whatsoever ye shall loose on earth shall be loosed in heaven.

Bind: Seducing Spirits (e.g., an infection)
Loose: The Holy Spirit - The Spirit of Truth
      (e.g., the antibiotic)

The warfare prayer:
(e.g., the instructions on how to take the antibiotic)

According to Matthew 16:19, I bind up the spirit of Seducing Spirits and every spirit that comes with the Seducing Spirits: Hypocritical Lies, Deception, Liar, Lured by False Prophets, Magic and the like, Lusts and Passions of the Flesh, Seducers, Enticers, Luring spirit of Evil (ways, objects or people) and any other spirit that is associated with the Seducing Spirits. Seducing Spirits, I bind you up from the root, according to the authority that God has given me in Matthew 16:19 and I loose according to Romans 8:13 and II Corinthians 6:7, the power of the Holy Spirit - the spirit of Truth in my life! I cast the spirit of Seducing Spirits and all of its spiritual attachments into the abyss - never to return! You are not welcomed in my life - my temple! No weapon formed against me shall prosper as God assures me in Isaiah 54:17! No Weapon! This I pray in the Name of Jesus!

It is also great to pray in the spirit at this point.

Now begin to worship our Father, for He is Almighty and worthy to be praised. Praise Him for the Victory! Praise God that you are completely guided by The Holy Spirit! Praise Him for His promised Word, in which He says that His word will not return unto Him void (Isaiah 55:11)!

SPIRIT OF LYING (e.g., an infection)

You are of your father, the devil, and it is your will to practice the lusts and gratify the desires [which are characteristic] of your father. He was a murderer from the beginning and does not stand in the truth, because there is no truth in him. When he speaks a falsehood, he speaks what is natural to him, for he is a liar [himself] and the father of lies and of all that is false (John 8:44).

The branches on the spiritual tree of the Spirit of Lying:

1. **Deception**: Acts 13:10; 2 Thessalonians 2:10; James 1:22
2. **Flattery**: I Thessalonians 2:3-6
3. **Religious Bondages**: Galatians 5:1-8; Romans 3:22-27; I Corinthians 6:11-12; I Corinthians 7:21
4. **Superstitions**: 1 Timothy 4:7
5. **False Prophesy**: Jeremiah 14:14; Jeremiah 23:16 Jeremiah 23:26; Micah 2:11 (8-11: The Message)
6. **Accusations and Judgment**: Job 27:5; Luke 23:14; Matthew 7:1-2; Luke 6:37; John 5:30; John 3:17-18; John 5:22; John 7:24; John 8:15
7. **Lies**: Proverbs 6:16-18
8. **Gossip**: Romans 1:29; I Timothy 5:13; I Timothy 3:11; 2 Timothy 2:16
9. **Slander and Backbiting**: Proverbs 10:18; Proverbs 26:22; Luke :65; I Timothy 6:4
10. **False Teachers**: 2 Corinthians 3:1; Galatians 3:18; 2 Peter :1

When is the spirit of Lying most likely to present itself during your spiritual pregnancy? Lying may present itself at anytime there appears to be an open door. Pay close attention to Religious Bondages, False Prophesy, Gossip, Accusations and Judgment as specified below:

1.   **Religious Bondages**: Period of Conception
2.   **Gossip, Accusations and Judgment, Slander and Backbiting**: All Periods
3.   **False Prophesy**: 2nd

NOTE: Although there are periods specified, understand that you may have evidence of these spirits (symptoms) at anytime during your spiritual pregnancy. Listed for your reference are the periods in which there most commonly noticed. It may vary from pregnancy to pregnancy and person to person.

Ye are of your father Satan, and the lusts of your father ye will do. He was a murderer from the beginning, and abode not in the truth, because there is no truth in him. When he speaketh a lie, he speaketh of his own: for he is a liar, and the father of it. (John 8:44)

I believe the spirit of Lying is one of the most commonly accepted spirits. There's white lies, big lies, tall lies, subconscious lies, lies with good cause, lies because "you've "gotta" do what you "gotta" do," lies to save the deal, lies to protect, gossip, slander, accusations, etc. It is so accepted in the world today, there's even gossip television shows and magazines, etc.

Just to give you an example of a few common, very accepted lies in the world. Even amongst God's children are the lies of Santa Clause, the Tooth Fairy, and the Easter Bunny; all for the *"joy of our children"*. As I look back on the lies told for the "cause", I can only speak for myself, but I never thought of these lies as a big deal. Now I think to myself how very interesting it is that the enemy has been able to deceive the majority with these "good cause" lies. The bottom-line is that NO LIE is acceptable in the eyes of God, NO LIE! According to John 8:44, Satan is the father of "ALL" lies.

According to The American College Dictionary, **lie** is defined as: "1. A false statement deliberately presented as being true; a falsehood. 2. Something meant to deceive or give a wrong impression." To lie is to deliberately deceive, which means since deceit is also on the evil tree of Seducing Spirits, in conjunction with the evil tree of Lying you also invite the Seducing Spirits and its entourage into your life as well. This now means that you have

149

more to battle on your road to attaining your *True Purpose*.

Another common area of lying is the spirit of flattery and it is often times overlooked. According to the American College Dictionary, **flattery** means: "Excessive or insincere praise." How many times have you praised someone for something and you knew in your heart that you were not sincere? In one breath you said to their face that you felt they did well or looked great and when they walked away, you thought to yourself or said to someone next to you, "Oh my goodness that was horrible!" Or, you know the ole, "Your baby is so... cute." But you feel otherwise. I know, you may think that's just trying not to hurt someone's feelings. Well, in fact that's a spirit of Lying that you are justifying or over-looking. It is better to be quiet when you don't have something good to say. Be of few words (Ecclesiastes 5:2).

Let's keep it real, there is such a fine line when it comes to lying. As the Lord begins to reveal these things to me so that you may receive this message, I say to myself, "WOW". Nonetheless, the enemy will turn up the dial a few notches on his offensive attacks against you as a result of your "Yes" to this spiritual process. As a result, this is the raw truth that "we" all must stomach and commit to change. You must increase your knowledge of this spiritual war so that you may stand defensively against the attacks of the enemy.

Satan is aware that you're depending on the guidance of the Holy Spirit (the *"voice"* of God). He knows that your spiritual pregnancy is intangible and as you read earlier, he will try your faith (your confidence in God's Word to you). He anticipates being successful at deceiving you in this process so that you can question the voice of the Holy Spirit, eventually causing you to question your faith, which may result in a spiritual abortion. By allowing the spirit of Lying to rein in your life, you "give place" to Deception and Seducing Spirits and you impede the progress of the Holy Spirit in your life.

Religious Bondage (Period of Conception)

In the period of Conception, it is very important that you do not allow the Spirit of Religious Bondage to hold you back from the call that God has on your life. Remember, in God, there are no restrictions. You are free through the Righteousness of Christ (Galatians 5:1-8).

In Chapter 5 I addressed Religious Bondages via the subject of the Breastplate of Righteousness, which as you now read is a part of the Lying spirit. If you are guided by the spirit of Religious Bondage, you are subject to completely restricting the Holy Spirit to control your life as we are admonished to do

> There are many man-made rules and regulations that are not a part of God's regulations.

in Romans 8:5. I believe this is a very sensitive area of discussion. To touch on the subject of Religious Bondage, I'm required to speak on the man-made traditions and religious beliefs that are practiced within most Christian Denominations and Churches. I am guided by the Holy Spirit and as He leads me I must write. Therefore, I offer no apologies for the truth, I just pray that you pray for the wisdom, knowledge, and understanding provided under the power of the Holy Spirit to be upon you as you receive what the Holy Spirit is revealing through me.

There are many man-made rules and regulations that are not a part of God's regulations. Unfortunately, these regulations have restricted many of you from moving forward with the spiritual purpose that God has planned for you. For example, no pants for women, and no shorts for men, restrictions from the movies, women not being allowed to wear nail polish, and if you do, you can't wear red because you would then look like a whore, and so on and on. Although for many years such trivial regulations were established within the church, many churches have graduated from these restrictions. However, there still lies other bondages that are a part of the church that must be torn down and without being redundant, the Holy Spirit will expound on this revelation of required change.

More commonly, the myth that based on your *works* you are righteous, as you read in Chapter 5. For example, many believe that if you have done certain sins like fornication for instance, you have done the "ultimate" sin. As a result, you are no longer a child of God and must repent and rededicate your life to Christ. Another common myth: if you are in continual sexual sin, you are completely denounced from God until you reframe from your *sinful nature*. Or, if you don't go to this church or that church you are not the favored one. I could go on and on.

The *relationship* you are to have with God is personal. Does any of this sound like a personal relationship to you? Well, this concept of religious belief, based on works and man-made rules and traditions, brings upon religious bondages in many different areas. This is the reason that so... many people feel they are not worthy to be a "Christian" until they have come to terms that they must be perfect before God first before excepting Christ – willing to drop everything immediately upon acceptance of Christ into their lives. This concept of religious belief is the reason that many people feel that they are not even worthy to move forward with God's promises for their lives. Then again, this concept of religious belief is the reason that many people feel that God is not a God of love, but a God of condemnation and slavery, not freedom. This concept of religious belief is the reason that most "Christians" judge one another and "others". This concept of religious belief is the reason that many people refuse to accept Christ at this time in their lives!

Fortunately, this concept of religious belief is completely contrary to the Word of God and is a lie to restrict the Kingdom of God from the growth in which God wants it to be. God is a God of Love! Again, this concept of religious belief brings about condemnation, not love, nor freedom. I doubt this belief is practiced maliciously within the churches; rather, I believe that it is largely due to the lack of revelation, unfortunately. On the other hand, "the church" should be your focus for determination, but God alone. God more desires a *"personal relationship"* with you. OK... moving along...

You must recognize what it means to be bound. The American Heritage College Dictionary defines **bondage** as: "1. the state of one who is bound as a *slave* or serf. 2. A state of *subjection* to a force or an *influence*." I want to also take the definition of the suffix, **bond** from the same dictionary: "2. Confinement in prison; captivity..." When I read these definitions, it reminds me so much of what I felt prior to me realizing who God really was. I didn't realize that I was bond until I was free. I thought that the religious stronghold by which I was bound was just the conviction of God in my life. This was contrary to the reality. It was not until I was free that God was able to mold and shape me into who He wanted me to be. It was not until I was able to understand that the mothers and the Pastor of the church were not who I needed to solely lean on for guidance. Rather, they were there to assist me in case I fell as they received counsel from the Holy Spirit. However, I later learned that I was required to establish a *personal relationship* with God – the Holy Spirit, trusting "totally" in Him and His word to me, not the other way around.

Many of you know what I mean when I say, "If the Pastor said it, that settles it". You may attend church 5 times a week, but not realizing that you are caught up in religious tradition and you don't really know God for yourself. You're just following the rules that are told to you over the pulpit. Ask yourself, "Who am I in God?" The Pastor may have said it, but did God say it or restrict it? You must study to show yourself approved (2 Timothy 2:15).

Yes, God gives us shepherds - Ministers to lead the flock (e.g., our spiritual mothers and fathers). Although they may be considered your spiritual mother and father here on earth, you are to be ultimately guided by the Holy Spirit which means that your spiritual mother and father should not be opposed of that. Spiritual leaders are not to be to the congregation as Mary and Joseph were to Jesus when He was a child. In spite of Jesus' urgency to do as the Holy Spirit was leading Him, as indicated in Luke 2:48-49, He was a child and had to first obey His parents. Jesus said to them, in Luke 2:49, "...*How is that you had to look for me? Did you not see and know that it is necessary [as a duty] for Me to be in*

My Father's house and [occupied] about My Father's business?"
Mary and Joseph did not understand what Jesus was talking about
(Luke 2:50). Consequently, Jesus was required to submit to His
parents and He became habitually obedient. (Luke 2:49) *"And He
went down with them and came to Nazareth and was [habitually]
obedient to them; and his mother kept and closely and persistently
guarded all these things in her heart."*

When Jesus became of age, He was free to be completely
guided by the Holy Spirit (Matthew 4:1; Acts 10:38). Unfortunately,
within the religious doctrines, many people view their Pastors,
Parishioners, or Leaders as Jesus viewed His natural – legal parents
when He was a child. Again, if it is against your practiced doctrine,
or if your Pastor doesn't understand how God is leading you, you
become completely immerged into the concepts and beliefs or your
Leader, Pastor, or Parishioner. When Jesus became of age, He
became completely guided by the Holy Spirit (Acts 10:38; Luke
2:27). He was no longer under the responsibility to follow His
parents. Contrary of this process of obedience to the Holy Spirit is
opposite of God's divine order.

It has been about 15 years ago that I received the revelation that
I was clueless and was under a religious bondage. **Pause**: Please
understand that I am not implying that all churches with rules are
a part of a religious bondage. Any organization or business has
guidelines to follow if one chooses to be a part of your organization;
otherwise the organization would not have a strong foundation.
However, the guidelines of your organization should not contradict
the Word of God with regards to one's obligation to be guided
by the Holy Spirit in order to attain *True Purpose* and their life's

fulfillment.

Since that time there has been more and more "Non-Denominational" Churches established. The Non-Denominational Church that I've attended has fed me the Word of God and through the Ministry I've been enlightened, encouraged, and richly blessed by the Word of God. It is awesome, because there are no religious bondages, but I've been encouraged to be guided by the Holy Spirit. Yes, there are groups that I can participate in, like any organization, and I'm encouraged to help and serve the community. More importantly, I'm encouraged to build the Kingdom of God first and I'm a part of a spiritual family.

> Again, understand, although God has made you free, it is not to be taken advantage of (Galatians 5:13).

If you are a child of God, it's great to want to conjugate with other children of God - your spiritual siblings in a mutual place (e.g., becoming a member of an organization). Nonetheless, your life should be exemplary of God in you at all times. In any organization there should be a leader. A spiritual leader is typically considered to be your Pastor, Bishop, Priest, or Minister. More specific, these individuals are considered to be and some being actually called to be a natural spiritual mother and/or father. Whatever organization you choose to join, your Leader should not teach you things that are contrary to God's message to His children. Otherwise, there is no substance. Be sure that your Leader is truly being led by the Holy Spirit. If not, how can they begin to guide you?

In conclusion, NO ONE can bind what God has freed through

the righteousness of Christ! The Holy Spirit will convict you as you strive to live a holy life as Jesus did. Again, understand, although God has made you free, it is not to be taken advantage of (Galatians 5:13). By the power of the Holy Spirit you will be chastened. By God's grace and His grace alone are you saved! Hence, God's Love and His message should be ministered as He works on the hearts of men and modifies who He has created through revelation given by the Holy Spirit to each and every one of us here on earth. Let God do the work within His children. If someone seems to go astray, learn to pray for all. God looks on the heart, so who are you to look on anything else? God is a God of love, not condemnation and judgment.

Religious Bondage and the interpretation of the Law of Marriage

An additional religious bondage that has held many people from delivering their *True Purpose* is the misinterpretation of God's expectations regarding all marriage unions. I approach this topic with care because I do not want the interpretation that I am insinuating in any way that marriage is not a union that is honored and sacred in the eyes of God. I am also not implying that divorce is the answer for all problems that arise in a marriage, because it is God's desire and plan for marriage to be until death do you part (Matthew 19:6). When the Pharisees were questioning Jesus regarding marriage and divorce, Jesus said, *"Because of the hardness (stubbornness and perversity) of your hearts Moses permitted you to dismiss and repudiate and divorce your wives but from the beginning it has not been so [ordained]."* So yes, God's desire is for those that are joined together to stay together if it be the will of God. However, you must also recognize that not everybody that has been joined together in "Holy Matrimony" is a couple that "God" ordained from the beginning. I will briefly address specifically the myth that God requires all to stay married, regardless of any circumstance, in this era as when Jesus was speaking to the Pharisees, before the crucifixion (Matthew 19:3-11).

Many people get married for many different reasons. Unfortunately, decisions on marriages are not typically derived from the guidance of the Holy Spirit. I can imagine some of you saying, "Yea right, who does that?! Let's keep it real." I know; that's why over 50% of documented marriages fail today. Typically, everyone just goes with the flow, the flesh and how good it feels. In fact, most people marry the complete opposite of who God made for them. Many of you married common traits - the person may have reminded you of your mother or father, who was sexually appealing to you, who seemed right for your situation, for the children, etc. Some of you even married regardless of the red flags you saw prior to marriage and some of you couldn't tell the signs for whatever reason. Rarely do marriages occur as a result of divine appointment. As a result, there are many unhappy couples and many people that are unable to fulfill their *True Purpose* as a result of the marriage. Many of you are trying to make things work when you should really let the marriage go so that you can be in the position to establish *True Purpose* in your life.

As you've read, through Christ you were made free. Per the crucifixion, you are not bound by any law (Galatians 3:13)! Under the law, you were to remain married until death and you were considered to have committed adultery unless your partner died or committed infidelity. However, through the righteousness of Jesus

Christ, you are made totally free. You now belong to God as a result and are not bound by any law (Romans 7:1-6). If you married outside of the will of God and God admonishes you to move on, you must follow the guidance of the Holy Spirit. I will repeat, you are bound by no law and you must follow the voice of God.

NOTE: *God does take marriage seriously. In fact, when Jesus is speaking to the Pharisees, He told them that if they thought the rules were too tough than they shouldn't marry (Matthew 19:11-12). Marriage is not for everyone, but you are bound by no law and you are to be led by the Holy Spirit regarding your life and your situation* (Romans 7:6).

God is a God of love, so it is definitely not God's will for you to be bound in a situation of abuse for example! Yes, God can do all things and He can turn your situation around! However, it is not God's will for some of your situations to turn around, but rather for some of you to SEPARATE or DIVORCE. Otherwise, you are guilty of forcing something that was never the will of God from the beginning.

Some of you have allowed the spirit of religious bondage or your misunderstanding of God's expectations of you regarding your marriage to keep you from the ultimate freedom that He's provided you. You must understand that when you've done all you can do, which is to stand, you must use wisdom for you and your children if you have them, and act on the freedom that God has provided you through the sacrifice of Jesus Christ! Pray for wisdom and understanding regarding your situation. Accept that you are not bound. You are not enslaved, but you are free in every area of your life and this includes marriage!

Ask yourself: "Did God ordain this marriage, or did I?" If God put you together, you will be free in the Spirit - free to live in Total Victory, and you will be free of any situation of abuse (physical, emotional, or verbal). Understanding that the enemy may try your marriage at times even being in the will of God, you should stand in faith if God leads you to do so regarding your marriage. God is able to restore and renew your relationship. In any case, do whatever God is leading "you" to do!

Judgment, Gossip, Back-biting, Slander and Accusations: (All Periods)

You must watch out for Gossip, Accusations and Judgment in all periods of your pregnancy. By gossiping and making accusations about others, you are judging them and you will be judged in the likeness or even worse (Matthew 7:1). To judge anyone, is contrary to the Word of God written in the Holy Bible, where you are admonished to treat others how you want to be treated (Matthew 7:12; Psalm 106:3). This is also the opposite of Love as described in I Corinthians 13. God says for you to love your neighbor as yourself, and is repeated at least 10 times in the Holy Bible, in which, are Words the majority of you claim to *trust and believe* (Leviticus 19:18; Matthew 5:43, Matthew 19:19; Matthew 22:39; Mark 12:31; Mark 12:33; Luke 10:27; Romans 13:9; Galatians 5:14; James 2:8). Think for a moment, how many times have your actions been misinterpreted? Or, you did something that you felt was completely out of your character? I'm sure countless times.

Therefore, watch what you say or think about others. You have no clue of their hearts or why they are where they are in their life. Take a moment to look at self. What has derived your current circumstance?

Judgment

During your spiritual pregnancy, you must also be very careful to not judge actions of others because the enemy will definitely use other people as an offensive attack against you. Some of these people may be loved ones or even people that you retain for a service, etc. Please keep in mind that in this spiritual pregnancy, God is molding you to trust Him, which includes resting in Him. You must understand that if you are following His guidance, everything is in divine order.

I recently wrote an article, "Don't assume that it is the devil attacking, it may be God snatching". Depending on what period you are in during your spiritual pregnancy, what may appear to be the enemy using someone, may just be the necessary process or circumstance for your spiritual pregnancy. For example, if you are in the period of conception and the 1st period, you are more than likely experiencing God snatching.

You never know who God is using as an instrument in your spiritual pregnancy, so you should keep your mouth off of people! Do not judge anyone's actions regardless of their error! Instead, pray for them. God requires you to walk in love and that excludes judgment of any type (Ephesians 5:2; 2 John 1:6).

Also recognize that in this spiritual pregnancy, the enemy will often times use other people to come against you with the spirit of Deception or the spirit of Seducing Spirits. Thereby, many times, the individual doesn't realize there being used by the enemy because they are bound by the spirit of Deception (James 1:22). I pray for those who are under a Strong Spirit of Deception. This spirit is a stronghold that can tear you down completely and cause you to walk in a clueless state of mind. Consequently, this spirit of Deception will cause you to not see yourself, including your error. In wrestling with this spirit, most times it takes others to intercede on your behalf because you are not capable of even seeing the changes that you need to make in your life.

Gossip, Back-biting, Slander and Accusations

I find it quite pathetic how many of the children of God participate in gossip, backbiting, slander, and accusations. "You must watch what you say about people!" Again, the bible says to not judge, nor condemn, so that you will not be judged or condemned (Matthew 7:1)! Unfortunately, I've heard many children of God saying, "God says, you know them by their fruits", derived from the scriptures Matthew 7:16 and Matthew 7:20. However, many people have taken this scripture out of context and have used it as a justification to gossip, backbite, judge, slander, condemn, and even accuse. Contrary to how these scriptures have been used, the scriptures referenced, pertain to right judgment of your choices as it relates to your personal relationships or dealing with people: (e.g., Teachers, Pastors, Business Associates, "Prophets", Informants, Friends, etc.). God wants you to use good judgment so that you are not mislead, taken advantage of, etc. However, to judge ones faith, circumstance, or choices, Jesus clearly admonishes you in Matthew

7:1, *"Do not judge and criticize and condemn others, so that you may not be judged and criticized and condemned yourselves."* Let God lead you on your dealings, as you are led by the Holy Spirit, and apart from that, you should not judge! Keep your mouth and opinions off of people. This is a branch on the spirit realm tree of Lying that must be addressed!

Not too long ago, I heard that a celebrity supposedly had established a new faith and was misleading the world down the wrong path. I don't like to put my mouth on someone else's situation because I don't know why that person is where they are in philosophy, faith, decision, or circumstance in life, and I don't want to have to find out why they are wherever they are, good or bad. However when I heard of this, I *was* curious to hear what the celebrity had to say about their faith. I feel that it is better to hear from the source rather than from someone else. So I went on-line where I was told there was information.

Unfortunately, I was more embarrassed and sickened by the information that I saw from the "children of God" with regards to this person's spiritual position, than the information regarding the celebrity's new found "faith". Before I could see the information, I must have seen countless gossip and judgmental comments and articles written and produced by the "children of God". I was disgusted! I thought to myself, it is a wonder many don't want to be a part of "our family"! Instead of some children of God using wisdom and knowledge, they slandered a soul. On behalf of the children of God, "Please forgive us, for those that have slandered you know not what they do."

Consider this: Imagine yourself a child living in a subdivision and one of the families down the street was supposedly the more fortunate family residing in the sub. Well you were confused as to where people got there information because you've actually spent a lot of time with the children that live in that house. You've seen the children fighting and talking about each other to other children residing in the sub. You've heard the children talking negatively about other children. You've had to tell them yourself, "Hey, that's not nice." You're thinking to yourself, "What kind of parents must these children have? Don't they teach them love?" You're thinking to yourself, "If that's fortunate, I want no parts of it. If the children are like that, I don't even want to meet the parents." Can you imagine that? God says through love and kindness have I drawn thee (Jeremiah 31:3). Where is the love amongst the children of God (the members of the Christ Movement)?

Another slander and judgment was done against a spiritual brother. He was slandered because He ministered the unconditional love of God, even for an Atheist. Remember, God looks at the heart! This brother stated that He didn't know if this person would go to "Hell" or would be "Eternally Damned" because He couldn't judge their heart. Guess what? He was right. You have no knowledge as to why the Atheist is an Atheist; nor, if they've accepted Christ at one time and have gone astray for whatever reason. Regardless of ones current position in faith, only God knows if that person is His child? If you know of an Atheist, say a prayer and leave the rest to God. According to the Holy Bible, on behalf of the children of God, "My spiritual brother, please forgive us, for those that have slandered you, know not what they do."

I ministered to an Atheist once, and this woman is now a believer. Guess what? She didn't believe God as a result of her circumstances. She believed that if it were a God than she wouldn't be where she was and per our initial conversation, she was adamant in her position. She didn't know of God's love or how to approach God. God gave me wisdom and love on how to minister to her. Through me, He met her where she was. She calls God her *Daddy* now. In my speaking to her, it was recognized that she was merely seeking love and could not find it. This perception as God being her Daddy has drawn her closer to God and gave her something to hold on to and to build a relationship from.

Keep your mouth off of people! Again, keep your mouth off of people! Pray for them and show them Love! Judge not so that you will not be judged (Matthew 7:1)!

Now, once you recognize that God is the righteous one and you're shinning in "His" Glory, you can better deliver His purpose and truly give Him all of the Glory and others may see God through you. But, you must be very careful to pay close attention to all of the fine detail with regards to the opposition in the Spirit Realm. The spirit of lying is treacherous to your elevation in *True Purpose*. You can not afford for this spirit to have any part in your life, so you must understand all of the ways that it can enter and you must stay conscious of its devices.

False Prophesy: 2nd Period

In the 2nd period, if you are not careful you can fall prey to the spirit of False Prophesy out of your eagerness to hear from God regarding His plan for your life. By now, you've just gotten pass the 1st Period which is the period that God was pruning you. You more than likely battled with confusion, depression, and anxiety because you DIDN'T KNOW what was going on. You may have also had frequent spouts of what seemed like silence from God regarding your direction. As you've moved on to the 2nd Period of your spiritual pregnancy, it feels really good to finally begin to receive clarity; however, you must be careful!

In your excitement for the clarity you've received you are very vulnerable and the enemy knows this. Therefore, you are open bait to be fed some news that parallels to the vision that you believe you see from false sources. Pace yourself! Pay close attention and keep in mind that this is the period of Listening and Following Instructions from "God". You're building a "personal relationship" with "God" and this period is the catalyst for that accomplishment! This is the period when you must definitely meditate more. You must not get too happy with every word that comes out of the mouth of man regarding your life, especially in this period (you'll recognize this period shortly after you've received some clarity and have just overcome a major hurdle in your life [via the result of transition or turmoil]).

I don't care how the word, information or informant seems to parallel to what you believe is God's will for your life, qualify your source with the Holy Spirit, the Spirit of God within you! This is crucial! How do you qualify? It can be approached several ways: In your spirit ask God, "Is this you?" Ask God for confirmation and God will give you a confirmation in your Spirit (the strongest feeling) and for some, an audible voice. Remember Proverbs 16:3 and roll your works over to God and know that He will cause His desires to become yours once you've done this. Keep in mind that the main accomplishment that must take place as a result of this spiritual pregnancy is a closer relationship, confidence and trust in "God" so that you can discover the mysteries regarding your life's fulfillment. God wants you to learn how to depend on His word to you. He wants to give you profound direction, wisdom, insight, understanding and peace for your life! You have to "know that you know that you know what you know", as I often say, and you can only have the confidence in knowing via the guidance of God's Spirit within you.

NOTE: This is not to say that God will not use people to give you a word. However, you must qualify the word. Take it with a grain of salt regardless of how good it sounds to you. Ask God for confirmation and He will give it to you in your Spirit.

How to destroy the spirit of Lying and every branch on its tree:

According to Matthew 16:19:

> *Verily, I say unto you, whatsoever ye shall bind on earth shall be bound in heaven and whatsoever ye shall loose on earth shall be loosed in heaven.*

Bind: Lying Spirit (e.g., the infection)
Loose: The Spirit of Truth and plead the Blood of Jesus over your life! (e.g., the antibiotic)

The warfare prayer:
(e.g., the instructions on how to take the antibiotic)

> *According to Matthew 16:19, I bind up the spirit of Lying and every spirit that comes with the Lying Spirit: Deception, Flattery, Religious Bondages, Superstitions, False Prophecy, Accusations, Lies, Gossip, Slander, and False Teachers. In the Name of Jesus, I bind up the Lying Spirit, from the root, according to the authority that God*

*has given me in His word and I loose according to John
14:17; 15:26; and 16:13 the Spirit of Truth! You Spirit of
Lying are not welcomed in my life! Lying Spirit, I bind you
and your entourage up and I cast you into the abyss, never
to return! No weapon formed against me shall prosper as
God assures me in Isaiah 54:17! No Weapon! For this I
pray and declare in the Name of Jesus!*

NOTE: It is also great to pray in the spirit at this point.

Now begin to worship our Father, for He is Almighty and Worthy to
be praised. Praise Him for the Victory! Praise Him that you walk in
TRUTH all the days of your life and the spirit of Lying has no place
in your life! Praise Him for His promised Word, in which He says
that His word will not return unto Him void (Isaiah 55:11)!

SPIRIT OF WHOREDOM (e.g., the infection)

A wicked and morally unfaithful generation craves a sign, but no sign shall be given to it except the sign of the prophet Jonah. Then He left them and went away (Matthew 12:39).

Read Jonah 1-3.

The branches on the tree of the Spirit of Whoredom:

1. **Unfaithfulness, Adultery**: II Chronicles 30:7; Proverbs 5:19; Jonah 1:1-10 (Suggestion: Read Chapters 2-4) Galatians 5:19; James 4:8; Matthew 12:39;   Matthew 16:4
2. **Lust of Money**: I Kings 3:5-14; II Chronicles 1:11-12; Proverbs 15:27; Proverbs 17:16; Ecclesiastes 7:12; James 4:2-4; I Timothy 3:3; I Timothy 6:10; 2 Timothy 3:2;   Hebrew 13:5
3. **Idolatry**: I Chronicles 5:25; Ezekiel 16:15; I Kings 9:6 (9:1-9); Psalm 66:16; Psalm 81:9; Jeremiah 13:10; Daniel 3:14-18, 28; I Corinthians 10:7
4. **Fornication**: Ezekiel 16:15; Acts 15:29; Acts 21:25; Galatians 5:19; Ephesians 5:3; I Corinthians 6:13, 18, I Corinthians 7:2; James 4:2-4; I Thessalonians 4:3 (4:1-5); I Timothy 3:3; I Timothy 6:10; 2 Timothy 3:2; Hebrews 13:5
5. **Spirit, Soul, or Body Prostitution**: Ezekiel 16:28; Romans 6:12; Romans 13:14; I Corinthians 6:20; I Corinthians 7:23; Matthew 22:37
6. **Worldliness**: James 4:4; I Chronicles 5:25; Psalm 81:8-13; Romans 1:31; John 15:19; John 17:23; I John 2:15

When is the spirit of Whoredom most likely to present itself during your spiritual pregnancy? Whoredom may present itself at anytime there appears to be an open door. Pay close attention to Worldliness; Idolatry; Body, Spirit and Soul Prostitution, Unfaithfulness, and Adultery as specified below:

1. **Spirit, Soul, or Body Prostitution, Fornication, Unfaithfulness, Adultery**: All Periods
2. **Idolatry, Love of Money**: Transition between 1st Period and 2nd Period
3. **Worldliness**: 1st Period and 2nd Period

NOTE: Although there are periods specified, understand that you may have evidence of these spirits (symptoms) at anytime during your spiritual pregnancy. Listed for your reference are the periods in which there most commonly noticed. It may vary from pregnancy to pregnancy and person to person.

Body, Spirit and Soul Prostitution, Fornication, Unfaithfulness, Adultery: All Periods

According to the American College Dictionary, ***whoredom*** is defined as: "'1. Prostitution.' '2a. Unlawful sexual relationships.' '3. Unfaithfulness to God; idolatry.'" This is a very strong definition. It is so crucial for you to understand this area and for you to not misinterpret nor eliminate any fraction of what the Holy Spirit is instructing me to admonish you.

According to the Holy Bible, fornication and adultery are sins that are "abominations-a strong disgust" to God (Ezekiel 11:18; Ezekiel 1:21). If you are a child of God, it is true that you are "not guilty" of sin as a result of the sacrifice made through Jesus Christ. As a result, you become the righteousness of Christ and are a child of God. According to I Corinthians 6:12 (Amplified Version),

Everything is permissible (allowable and lawful) for me; but not all things are helpful (good for me to do, expedient and profitable when considered with other things). Everything is lawful for me, but I will not become the slave of anything or be brought under its power.

Oh my...I can vision some of you with your mouth wide open. Its OK, read further so that you may gain thorough knowledge of what the Holy Spirit has to reveal to you.

NOTE: the reason for you not committing sin should not be for the possibility of "damnation". It should be, however, for the "love" of God and for your desire to please Him and for you to offer a greater possibility and life of fulfillment for yourself, your children, and others. Your decisions today determine opposition and success for your children not just in the natural, but even more so in the spirit realm. Remember: you conquer spirit realm, you conquer life! Continuing...

As long as you remain here on this earth, as a child of God, you are required to be guided by the Holy Spirit and not by the flesh (Romans 8:4). You are required to live a life of holiness and to follow after the example of Jesus Christ (I Peter 2:1). Nevertheless, as long as you are alive you will wrestle in the spirit realm, against principalities and the rulers of darkness (Ephesians 6:12). Therefore in this spiritual war, it is very important that you remain aware of the enemy's attempt to take advantage of you in every way possible. One key trick the enemy has used is the lust of the flesh, which is what derives the operation of whoredom. Through the lust of the flesh, the enemy has been able to plant great temptations in the lives of many; thereby, resulting in horrible cycles in one's personal life and in families for generations.

In I Corinthians 6:12, Paul could not have said it better: *not all things are helpful.* Through the door of sexual sin, you partake of a sexual soul-tie. According to the American Heritage College Dictionary, *soul* is defined: "A person's emotional or moral nature; the animating and vital principle in human beings, credit with the faculties of thought, action, and emotion ..." From the same dictionary, ties is defined as: "To confine or restrict; to equal; something that connects or unities (marital ties)."

In I Corinthians 6:16, "Or do you not know and realize that when a man joins himself to a *prostitute, he becomes one body with her? The two, it is written, shall become* **one flesh.**" According to the American Heritage College Dictionary, the word **fornication** means, "Sexual intercourse between partners who are not married to each other." Fornication is derived from the "Latin word (*fornix*, from which *fornication*, the ancestor of *fornication*, is derived, meant "a vault, an arch." The term also referred to *a vaulted cellar where prostitutes plied their trade.* This sense of fornix in Late Latin yielded the verb *fornicari*, "to commit fornication," from which is derived *fornication*, whoredom, fornication."

> Through the lust of the flesh, the enemy has been able to plant great temptations in the lives of many; thereby, resulting in horrible cycles in one's personal life and in families for generations.

Spiritually, the "body" is defined as the temple of the Holy Spirit which is a Spirit. Hence, this joining (tie) is a spiritual tie; not one of the flesh as in a marriage (I Corinthians 6:19). As a child of God, according to I Corinthians 6:20, you were bought with a price. Therefore, to fornicate or to offer your body as a prostitute (fornicate), you are selling yourself short to the enemy. According to the American College Dictionary, **prostitute** is defined in one instance, "To sell for an unworthy purpose." **Prostitution** is defined as, "The act or an instance of offering or devoting one's talent unworthily."

Although in this scripture Paul was speaking of joining with a person in the flesh, it is clear that if your body, the temple of the Holy Spirit becomes one then your spirit also becomes one. Consequently, the act of sex results in a joining (tie) that binds two people together in the spirit realm. Thus, whatever your partner has spiritually, rather it is good or bad, you invite into your body (your temple). Regardless if you are married or not, sexual intercourse is an open door for Satan and his entourage to invade your life; which is a major reason why you'd want to be careful who you have sex with and definitely who you marry (become as one in the flesh). God says that we are to be led and "guided" by the Holy Spirit and if you are partaking in fornication, promiscuity, or are unfaithful to God [adultery and idolatry], you are being controlled by the flesh (Romans 7:5; 8:5, 13:14).

Before I move on from this topic, I want you to get a visual of this in the spirit realm. You worry about STDs in the natural, but the spiritual bondages that can enter your life as a result of intercourse are way more frightening. Imagine this: Every time you have intercourse with "anyone", the enemy uses that opportunity to inject you with evil spirits as a dope pusher would use a syringe to inject dope in your veins. In other words, this is the enemy's opportunity to build up the opposing team that will work against you.

When you are married, it is as if you're wearing a rubber in the natural. In the spirit realm there is a hedge of protection over you as a result of your vow made before your partner and God. God honors and protects that union for as long as it remains. Although you are still subjected to the spirits of your spouse, you are under the protection of the Holy Spirit per this vow between your partner and God (Hebrew 13:3). This prevents the enemy from having full reign in your life. On the other hand, if you are committing fornication or adultery, it is as if you are performing sexual intercourse with no protection in the natural. Consequently, you are subjected to many more bondages (a much more potent injection from the enemy), which means you have much more to battle in the spirit realm during your spiritual pregnancy. (As if you need to battle anything else.)

I don't want to paint the picture that God is not protecting all of His children, because He is and we all have sinned and fallen short of the glory of God (Romans 3:23). So, why is there a greater consequence? For one, according to the Word of God, *fornication* is an abomination to God, which means that it is a disgust; a strong dislike to Him. Again, a root of fornication is prostitution, which is "the act or an instance of offering or devoting one's talent unworthily." Hence, you sell yourself short of the promise and your opportunity for *True Purpose* (complete fulfillment) in your life. Once you realize that God's plan for you is that you have a life of fulfillment, peace, love, joy, and freedom, you will understand why this is a disgust to Him. This defeats His purpose and plan for you. Not to mention the additional spiritual battle that you are bound to face as a result of fornication.

A second way to look at this is in a parent-child scenario. If you had 2 children and you told both of them to not lean back in the chair, but one child decides to deliberately disobey you and the other child accidently falls, what would be your response to the child that disobeyed you? I'll share with you what I would do in such a scenario. More than likely, I would not immediately run to the rescue of the disobedient child, depending on the danger of the fall. Although, the child may cry and feel they've severely injured themselves, I would use that opportunity to reiterate the reason I told them not to lean back in the chair in the first place. Hopefully, the child would not make the decision to not lean back in the chair again and learn from the mistake. As for the child that was not disobedient, I would more than likely catch the child before the chair hit the ground.

Moving right along…Rather you are rich and in great health, or living a comfortable life and you've accomplished all of the dreams that you could ever imagine, if you are allowing your flesh to control you, and you are committing the act of fornication or adultery, you haven't begun to see what God could do through you without these spiritual hindrances – this sexual bondage. Believe me, there is an even greater level that God would take you beyond your wildest dreams. This dream will not only bring joy and fulfillment to your life, but others as well. Currently, you see fulfillment through the flesh – your current reality; however, if you will allow yourself to be completely guided by the Holy Spirit, God will show you His reality that is already planned for you. You think you're there now, imagine where you could be. I know, you can't, and that's the point.

To summarize: Regardless of your natural protection, every time you have intercourse, you are being injected spiritually and aligning yourself in the spirit realm with your sexual partner (married, or unmarried). If you're committing sexual sin, fornication or adultery, view the enemy with a syringe in his hand full of demonic spirits as he's injecting you with his dirty needle. (And you thought STDs were bad?) What a way to look at this. I don't know about you, but when I got this revelation, it changed my view of sexual intercourse.

Some of you may wonder why after you've ended a bad relationship, you find yourself in another relationship that was the same or worse than the one you had before. Well, your spirit is attracted to the spirit that had you bound before; rather the familiar spirit came as a result of your relationship or a result of your family blood-line. Now do you see the importance of being sure that you are equally yoked "spiritually" with your partner? (II Corinthians 6:14). Of course you don't know of someone's spiritual trail; but, if you ask God to show you a person's spirit, He will. A benefit of being completely guided by the Holy Spirit is that He promises to teach you all things.

In the spirit realm, you have enough to battle from your blood-line, the spirits that feel entitled to you via familiarity. The last thing you need is to have to deal with someone else's familiar spirits or invited spirits that are in their life. This is not good for you in spiritual battle and definitely not in this spiritual pregnancy.

In the natural, women are advised to not do certain things while they're pregnant due to the side effects that it may cause to their unborn child. In the spirit realm, there are some things that you should not do as a result of the side effects it will cause during your spiritual pregnancy – the road to attaining *True Purpose* in your life. The only way that you can fulfill the purpose that God has called for you is to be completely guided by the Holy Spirit. Therefore, respect the temple of God and don't allow your flesh to control you. Consequently, you minimize unwanted spiritual guest as well as unwanted circumstances in your life.

Idolatry: Period of Conception and 1st Period

I won't forget when the Holy Spirit gave me the revelation that if you are not doing as God has called you to do, you are worshiping other gods. To allow the spirit of idolatry to take control in your life you open the door to every spirit on this spirit realm tree. He said to me, "You are to have no other god before me (Exodus 20:3; 34:14)". Prior to the Holy Spirit showing me this, I would have never considered that not doing what I was called to do here on earth as idolatry. I viewed other gods as if I prayed to someone other than Jehovah, God. However, I realized at this point, it was much more real than how I had initially interpreted.

Some of you may resist more than others in these periods because you may be required to go into a direction that your flesh is not anticipating. However, if you choose to go in the opposite direction of where God is calling you, you are yielding to the spirit of Idolatry - worshiping other gods (Psalm 106:39).

Worldliness: 1st Period and 2nd Period

I need to make clear the phrase, "love not the things of this world". Understand that if you are striving towards anything aside the call of God via job, house, material things, relationship or whatever it is, consider it to be "worldly" and it is not of God! For example, many people have considered individuals with what is considered to be the finer things in life as being worldly. However, this is not true. God may have ordained for one person (and it doesn't mean that God has respect of person) to have a big house on a hill and no need to work everyday and for another person to have a home considered to be middle class and a decent 9 to 5 job. God has everything in divine order and He has placed us in all different parts of the earth with a purpose to minister to people all over the world on all different levels.

If all of God's children were on the hill, what would happen to the people that were on ground level? The bottom-line is that you can't focus on the "things" of this world, but rather the call of God for your life. As a result, God will make His desires become yours as He promises you in Proverbs 16:3. Remember this: To whom much is given much is required. Trust and believe that if God ordained for someone to be on the hill or to have a billion dollars, for example, there is a major requirement within the earth to be fulfilled that is far beyond what you could probably imagine or even desire to have for a responsibility of your own. Be grateful where you are and keep your eyes on God. In the obedience of God you'll find peace, satisfaction and TOTAL VICTORY!

***

The presence of this spirit may be very strong in some pregnancies; in many cases, making it appear as though the opportunities in the world are more fruitful or attractive than the things of God. According to I John 2:15-17:

Love not the world, neither the things that are in the world. If any man loves the world, the love of the Father is not in him. For all that is in the world, the lust of the flesh, and the lust of the eyes, and the pride of life, is not of the Father, but is of the world. And the world passeth away, and the lust thereof.

What does this tell you? First, only what you do for God will last. Second, you are to deny the opportunities of the world - choose to not commit idolatry. Third, follow God's plan at all cost! Remember, God says that if you roll all of your works over to Him, your plans will be established and succeed (Proverbs 16:3)!

Love of Money: Transition between 1st period and 2nd Period

Many of you are seeking Purpose to find stability or wealth. In other words, you're pimping God for what He can offer you because "God said in His word that I can ask what I will and it will be done unto me, so…" On the other hand, many of you are using God as an investment opportunity – paying tithes because "God said that if I pay my tithes I'll get 100 fold." I guess you could consider this, pimping God's Love and His Word, "God said that His word would not return unto Him void." Some may also say aloud. The worse part is, when you don't get your return back fast enough, the enemy uses this as an opportunity to plant seeds of doubt in your mind that may cause you to question the Word of God. God is not the stock market! Money should not be your motive and for this, God is not pleased.

It is not all about you, but it is about God and His glory. It's about His reign upon the earth which can only be accomplished through God's ability to work through you and many others! You're a vessel, a soldier, a child of the King here for a mission to be fulfilled. So make sure that your heart is in the right place and you're not guilty of pimping God. A great example is Solomon. When given an opportunity to get whatever he wanted from God, he asked for wisdom of how to begin and finish and how to have a discerning mind. (I Kings 3:5-9). Just like Jesus, Solomon's objective was to please God and as a result, God blessed him with riches (I Kings 3:10-14). (Read: I Kings 3 and 4).

As you transition from the 1st period to the 2nd period you will begin to see clearer the direction that God is sending you. At this time, you may also realize that your call doesn't come with a huge dollar sign ($) attached to it. For some, it may even mean that you down-size (sacrifice the things of this world) to go where God wants you. Unfortunately, for the Love of Money, many of you may deny the call of God and opt to commit idolatry. Hence, spiritually aborting the *True Purpose* that God ordained for the call of God for your life just to keep up appearances or your status quo.

So, it is necessary for you to realize that not everyone is called to be millionaires and billionaires. However, everyone must trust God and rest assure that if you do as God has called you and seek knowledge as Solomon did in I Kings, according to Philippians 4:19, God "WILL" provide all of your needs according to His riches in glory, and you will live a blessed and fulfilled life wherever you are as a result of your obedience (Matthew 13:12).

How to destroy the spirit of Whoredom and every branch on its tree:

According to Matthew 16:19:

Verily, I say unto you, whatsoever ye shall bind on earth shall be bound in heaven and whatsoever ye shall loose on earth shall be loosed in heaven.

181

Bind: Whoredom (e.g., the infection)
Loose: The Spirit of God, Pure Spirit (e.g., the antibiotic)

The warfare prayer:
(Instruction of how to take the antibiotic)

> *According to Matthew 16:19, I bind up the spirit of Whoredom and every spirit that comes with the spirit of Whoredom: Unfaithfulness; Adultery; Lust of Money; Idolatry; Judges; Fornication; Spirit, Soul, or Body Prostitution; and Worldliness. In the Name of Jesus, I bind up the spirit of Whoredom, from the root, according to the authority that God has given me in His word and I loose according to Isaiah 25:1 and Isaiah 65:16, the Spirit of God and a Pure Spirit in me! You are not welcomed in my life! Lying Spirit, I bind you and your entourage up and I cast you into the abyss, prohibiting you to ever return! No weapon formed against me shall prosper as God assures me in Isaiah 54:17! No Weapon! This I pray in the Name of Jesus!*

NOTE: It is also great to pray in the spirit at this point.

Now begin to worship our Father, for He is Almighty and worthy to be praised. Praise Him for the Victory! Praise Him that you are completely guided by the Holy Spirit and nothing or anything has control over your temple of God! Praise God that you are pure and holy! Praise Him for His promised Word, in which He says that His word will not return unto Him void (Isaiah 55:11)!

SPIRIT OF HAUGHTINESS - PRIDE (e.g., an infection)

Pride cometh before destruction and a haughty spirit before a fall (Proverbs 16:18).

The branches on the tree of the spirit of Haughtiness

1. **Pride**: Proverbs 6:16-17; 16:18-19; 28:25; Proverbs 8:13; Proverbs 29:23; Jeremiah 50:32; Mark 7:21-23; Romans 3:27; Romans 11:18; Ephesians 2:9; Philippians 3:3
2. **Deception**: John 7:18; Acts 13:10; 2 Thessalonians 2:10; James 1:22
3. **Idleness**: Exodus 5:17; Proverbs 10:4, 14:23, 19:15; 2 Thessalonians 3:11; Titus 1:10
4. **Scornful**: Matthew 18:10; I Timothy 6:2; Proverbs 15:12
5. **Arrogant, smugness**: Psalm 75:4; II Timothy 3:2; Jude 1:16
6. **Obstinate**: Exodus 9:12; Colossians 3:6; Titus 3:3
7. **Strife**: Proverbs 16:28; 17:1, 14, 19; I Timothy 6:4
8. **Contentious**: I Corinthians 11:16; Proverbs 27:15
9. **Rejection of God**: Luke 12:9; I Thessalonians 4:5-8
10. **Self-Righteousness**: Ephesians 4:24; Philippians 3:9
11. **Rebellion**: Proverbs 17:11; II Thessalonians 2:7; Hebrews 3:8, 13

When is the spirit of Haughtiness most likely to present itself during your spiritual pregnancy? Haughtiness may present itself at anytime there appears to be an open door. Pay close attention to Obstinate, Pride and Deception, Arrogant and Smugness as specified below:

1. **Obstinate**: Period of Conception
2. **Pride and Deception**: 1st Period, Period of Delivery, After Birth
3. **Arrogant, Smugness**: Period of Delivery and Labor, After Birth

NOTE: Although there are periods specified, understand that you may have evidence of these spirits (symptoms) at anytime during your spiritual pregnancy. Listed for your reference are the periods in which there most commonly noticed. It may vary from pregnancy to pregnancy and person to person.

Obstinate: Period of Conception and 1st Period

A very deadly area of pride is obstinate. According to www.dictionary.com, *obstinate* could not have been defined better: "1. Firmly, or stubbornly adhering to one's purpose..." The Merriam-Webster Dictionary defines *stubborn* as it relates to obstinate: "implies sturdiness in resisting change which may or may not be admirable (a person too stubborn to admit error)." With this spirit showing operable in your life, you can really have a difficult time conforming to this initial unknowing, unplanned, often times non-common sense of a direction for your life. It can be very difficult adjusting to the realm of *Revelation* rather than *Common-Sense*. God's revelation on direction doesn't necessarily make sense to man and if you are allowing the spirit of Obstinate to take control in your life, you will buck against the call of God.

You need a humble and contrite spirit (Isaiah 57:15). Not just humble to people, but also humble to the call of God, and it is guaranteed that God's call will definitely humble you! (Isaiah 2:11; 5:15; 10:33)! According to The American College Dictionary, *humble* is defined as: "1. Marked by meekness or modesty in behavior, attitude, or spirit; not arrogant or prideful. 2. Showing deferential or submissive respect." To be *humbled* means: "1. To curtail or destroy the pride of; humiliate. 2. To cause to be meek or modest in spirit. 3. To give a lower condition or station to; abase (to lower in rank)." The same dictionary defines *contrite* as: "1. Feeling regret and sorrow for one's sins or offenses; penitent."

What was one of the greatest attributes that you saw through the birth and death of Jesus? First, God humbled Himself as He gave of Himself and created in the flesh Jesus as His son so that we may have a living example of this profound process of life. Second, Jesus was humbled through His suffering. Jesus walked a humble life through to His death (Philippians 2:8)! How do you think God felt as His Son suffered the crucifixion? God could have allowed Jesus to pass early on in the process so there would not be too much suffering. However, He wanted us to understand and realize His love and the complete anointing of the sacrifice and the power in completion. So, it is about the call of God on your life and you attaining *True Purpose* at all cost! It is not about how you look in a situation: to your boss, to your family, to your friends. It is about God's plan being fulfilled in your life so that through your fulfillment, it will bear witness of God's goodness, mercy, and grace as it was witnessed through the life of Jesus! Do what God has called you to do. God said by humility and fear of the Lord are riches, honor, and life (Proverbs 22:4). In the end, God will get all of the glory and you will be exalted by God (James 4:10; I Peter 5:6).

Pride and Deception: 1st Period, Period of Delivery and After Birth

According to The American Heritage Dictionary, *pride* has several meanings: "1. A sense of one's own proper dignity or value; self-respect. 2. Pleasure or satisfaction taken in an achievement, a possession, or an association." On the other hand it defines pride as: "3. Arrogant or disdainful conduct or treatment; haughtiness." In the spirit realm, when I reference pride, I am referencing specifically how it is defined in #3. According to the Word of God in the Holy Bible, "pride" comes before destruction and "haughty" before a fall (Proverbs 16:18). In other words, if you are dangerously prideful or haughty, you are sure to fall or see destruction at some point in your life. This is not to say that everyone that suffers a down time is dealing with the spirit of Pride, because there are several periods in this spiritual pregnancy that you will be humbled and by what sometimes may appear as a decline or setback. According to Isaiah 2:11, *"The lofty looks of man shall be humbled, and the haughtiness of men shall be bowed down, and the LORD alone shall be exalted in that day."*

There's a thin line between an acceptable pride and a dangerous pride. For many that become high achievers and the wealthy, it can be very easy to venture to the dangerous side of pride because society will typically place you on a pedestal. Unfortunately, if you are not being guided by the Holy Spirit, it can be hard to distinguish between an acceptable and non-acceptable praise for oneself. However, as you allow yourself to be guided by the Holy Spirit you'll realize that it is not about you, it is about God. Therefore, it will become difficult to give acknowledgement to yourself without giving all of the glory first to God and doing this sincerely from your heart. You will grow so strong in the Spirit until you will not jump at opportunities to talk about what "you've done" or what "you have".

Unfortunately, many people don't realize that the spirit of Pride has control of them as a result of the spirit of Deception that is also on this spirit realm tree of Pride. Usually it is the period when God begins to prune you (the process of humbling) of all that you seemed to have control of in your life: the accolades, or, a loved one or something you love dearly, when you may finally come to realize the presence of this spirit of Pride.

When I think of humble, I'm reminded of the beautiful late Rosa Parks, a civil rights leader whose stand against racial discrimination stirred the civil rights movement across the nation. Even in her major stand, she didn't get violent, she humbly and sternly said what she meant and meant what she said. Her stand changed the world. Let me ask, "How many of you know that God was using her at that time and the boldness that she possessed at that time also came from God?" The stand she took could have cost her and her families life, which was eventually threatened as a result of her stand. Rosa Parks until now is known for her grace and her humbleness. She did not praise herself, people praised her and she gracefully received the praise.

A Government official, once said, "The woman we honor today, held no public office, she wasn't a wealthy woman, didn't appear in the society pages... and yet when the history of this country is written, it is this small, quiet woman whose name will be remembered long after the names of senators and presidents have been forgotten."

As I remember viewing her body, among the thousands from across the world that viewed her body, she looked like a porcelain doll. Many testified of how you could feel her humble, peaceful, and graceful spirit in the room where her body was shown. To even write of this, I get chills and tears fill my eyes. I say to God, "What an example Lord. I want to be as she was: humble and graceful." I want to be considered a "diamond polished in the hands of God" as Bishop Philip Robert Cousin of the AME Church described Mrs. Rosa Parks according to the American Press.

The Pharisee

The Pharisee took his stand ostentatiously and began to

pray thus before and with himself: God, I thank You that I am not like the rest of men--extortionists (robbers), swindlers [unrighteous in heart and life], adulterers--or even like this tax collector here. I fast twice a week; I give tithes of all that I gain. But the tax collector, [merely] standing at a distance, would not even lift up his eyes to heaven, but kept striking his breast, saying, O God, be favorable (be gracious, be merciful) to me, the especially wicked sinner that I am! (Luke 18:11-13)

After you've read these verses of scripture, you can hopefully understand how it can be very easy to take what you may call giving glory to God or using an opportunity to speak facts about your position or accomplishments as a segment to uplift what "you've done" or what "you've got" in a prideful manner.   The Pharisee stood "alone" and prayed in verse 11, *"God, I thank you that I am not like other people who steal, cheat, or take part in adultery, or even like this tax collector. I give up eating twice a week, and I give one-tenth of everything I get!"* If

> There's a thin line between an acceptable pride and a dangerous pride.

you notice, the Pharisee was talking to God like how you may talk to a buddy. "I'm glad that I'm not like Tim. At least I'm doing what God wants me to do and I go to church."

Now in the same breath that the Pharisee was giving "thanks to God", the Pharisee was proud about his position and what he felt he wasn't and how good he was in his giving, etc. Even in his prayer, he was giving glory to himself – boasting in his position. Obviously, he did not realize that it was only through the strength and ability that God gave him that he was able to accomplish whatever he accomplished. Otherwise, he would have used that opportunity to pray for those that he compared to himself. His prayer may have been something like:

> *"Father, in the name of Jesus, I thank you for your grace that you've given to me. Without you I would be nothing. Father, I pray for those that are short of grace. Have mercy on them and show them who you are in their life. Thank you Father."*

What's the word? Pray for those that fall short. It is only by the grace of God that you are where you are or have what you have.

Arrogant and Smugness: Delivery, Labor, and After Birth

In The American College Dictionary, *arrogant* is defined as: "1. Making or disposed to make claims to unwarranted importance or consideration out of overbearing pride." In the same dictionary, *smug* (the root word of smugness) is defined as: "1. Exhibiting or feeling great or offensive satisfaction with oneself or with one's situation; self-righteously complacent."

Once you've gone through your extensive spiritual pregnancy and labor, you should feel a sense of accomplishment for what God has given you the strength and ability to achieve. Although, you made the decision to be obedient to go after your *True Purpose*, it is important for you to remember that it was God that gave you the ability to see it through to fruition. Some of you are elevating to a level that even man may want to give you praise as a result of your achievement, which is fine. However, what you must maintain is a humble nature and a stable ground in God abiding in and with Him at all times so that you don't become "self-righteously complacent".

The Bitter-Sweet Elevation

You are to be humble in your elevation (James 1:9). Regardless of what you've accomplished, it is God that gave you the ability. Whatever rewards or accolades you receive as a result of the accomplishments, remain humble and focused on God so that He may always receive the glory for what has been done through you. Nonetheless, I do understand that some of you are called by God to be financially wealthy. Needless to say, for you to get to that point or to have gotten to this point, you most likely have experienced or will experience much persecution on the way up the ladder. As I always say, "The higher the call, the harder the challenge." If you have not made it to your point of wealth yet, you will most likely lose before you gain, regardless of the presence of the spirit of Haughtiness or not. Just when you thought you were humble, you will be humbled some more. The last thing God needs is a "haughty-wealthy" child of God.

You may have noticed, most of the success stories of those that are very wealthy and proclaiming to be God fearing, generally have stories of poverty, or some sort of suffering just prior to elevation? This is not to say that ungodly people don't get to financial abundance, but remember, the wealth of the sinner is laid up for the just (Proverbs 13:22). Not to mention, according to I John 2:17, only what you do for God will last. Continuing on…

In this process, it is very necessary for you to remain sweet to even the people that will turn their backs on you when you're down. It is important to remain in love with the people that don't understand. Show them the love of God and the example Jesus Christ gave to us. Give them the love that passes all human knowledge and understanding. (Ephesians 3:19). Understand this: people don't have the vision that you have. Remember: God has revealed this impossible thing to you not them. Therefore, not everyone will understand, see, or believe your vision as you climb up the ladder. As a matter of fact, you'll be surprised, who won't believe in you - many people will not believe in what you're doing.

Delivery

The closer you get to the end, the more the enemy will use people to show disbelief in what you've believed God for in your life. You'll probably look crazy to many people. If you've been brought to the point where you're not financially where you once were, you must remain humble and not get the attitude, "I can't wait until things come through for me; I won't forget anything that they've done to me", or, "I'll remember this and they had better not ask me for anything."

After-Birth

What is your thought for those that didn't believe in you? What happens if they come back after you've made it? I strongly suggest, so that you are not a partaker of the spirit of Haughtiness, you will do as Jesus would do…continue to be humble. You will not do the, "I told you so" or take an opportunity to arrogantly talk about what you have and how you've gotten to where you were striving. No! You are going to remain humble and continue to walk in love. Trust me, whatever God wanted them to see as a result of your elevation and the disbelief they had in the beginning, the Holy Spirit has already informed them. Besides, every attack that is allowed from the enemy is only to make you stronger!

How to destroy the spirit of Haughtiness and every branch on its tree:

According to Matthew 16:19:

Verily, I say unto you, whatsoever ye shall bind on earth shall be bound in heaven: and whatsoever ye shall loose on earth shall be loosed in heaven.

Bind: Haughtiness (e.g., the infection)
Loose: Humble and Contrite Spirit – Psalm 34:2 and
Psalm 25:9 (e.g., the antibiotic)

The warfare prayer:
(Instruction of how to take the antibiotic)

According to Matthew 16:19, I bind up the spirit of Haughtiness and every spirit that comes with the spirit of Haughtiness: Pride; Deception; Scornful; Idleness; Arrogance, Smugness; Obstinate; Strife; Contentious; Rejection of God; Self-Righteous; Rebellion. In the Name of Jesus, I bind up the spirit of Haughtiness from the root, according to the authority that God has given me in Matthew 16:19, and I loose according to Psalm 25:9 and Psalm 34:2, a Humble and Contrite Spirit! Spirit of Haughtiness, you are not welcomed in my life! Haughtiness, I bind you and your entourage up and I cast you into the abyss, prohibiting you to ever return!

No weapon formed against me shall prosper as God assures me in Isaiah 54:17! No Weapon! This I pray in the Name of Jesus!

NOTE: It is also great to pray in the spirit at this point.

Now begin to worship God, for He is Almighty and worthy to be praised. Praise Him for the Victory! Praise Him that you are completely guided by the Holy Spirit and nothing or anything has control over your temple of God! Praise God that you are humble and contrite! Praise Him for His promised Word, in which He says that His word will not return unto Him void (Isaiah 55:11)!

SPIRIT OF SLOTHFULNESS (e.g., an infection)

The slothful man does not catch his game or roast it once he kills it, but the diligent man gets precious possessions. (Proverbs 12:27)

The branches on the tree of the spirit of Slothfulness:

1. **Slothful, Laziness and Indolence**: Proverbs 26:14; Proverbs 12:24; 19:15; 15:19, 19:24

2. **Idleness**: Proverbs 10:24; Ezekiel 16:49; II Thessalonians 3:1

3. **Sluggish**: Proverbs 10:24; Proverbs 26:16; Hebrews 6:12

4. **Poverty**: Proverbs 20:13; 23:21; 10:15; 13:18

When is the spirit of Slothfulness most likely to present itself during your spiritual pregnancy? The spirit of Slothfulness may present itself at anytime there appears to be an open door. Pay close attention to Slothfulness, Indolence, and Laziness as specified below:

1. **Slothfulness and Indolence**:
   1st Period and Period of Delivery
2. **Laziness**: 2nd Period

NOTE: Although there are periods specified, understand that you may have evidence of these spirits (symptoms) at anytime during your spiritual pregnancy. Listed for your reference are the periods in which there most commonly noticed. It may vary from pregnancy to pregnancy and person to person.

In the natural, many women experience extreme fatigue in the 1st trimester of pregnancy as the body adjusts to the hormonal changes as a result of the pregnancy. Personally, I experienced this extreme fatigue and for two and a half months I could barely make it through a days work, less alone anything else, like the chores around the house. This was not very productive for me or my family. In the spirit realm, after you take the step towards implementing *True Purpose* in your life, the enemy will not appreciate your effort and will challenge your productivity. One major area the enemy can attack productivity is through slothfulness.

As you already know, words are powerful as I've demonstrated to you in this book. According to the Holy Bible, "life and death" are in the power of the tongue (Proverbs 18:21). Occasionally, I will dissect a word to bring notice to the strength in that word. I like you to understand that not all the time when you are saying one word, you're saying one word. Often times, you're saying 20 that all together is more powerful than you ever could imagine. So that you may obtain a thorough understanding of what you're dealing with if you allow the spirit of "Slothfulness" to partake in your life, I must dissect this word.

According to The American Heritage College Dictionary, *slothful* is defined: "1. Aversion to work or exertion; laziness; indolence." *Exert* is defined: "1. To put to use or effect; put forth. 3. To put (oneself) to strenuous effort." *Laziness* is defined: "1. Resistance to work or exertion; disposed to idleness. 2. Slow-moving; sluggish... 3. Conducive to idleness or indolence." *Indolence* is defined: "1. Habitual laziness; sloth."; or, indolent: "1a. Disinclined to exert oneself; habitually lazy. b. Conducive to inactivity or laziness; lethargic." *Idle* is defined: "2. Lacking substance, value, or basis.", "2. To move lazily without purpose." Finally, *sluggish* is defined: "3. Slow to perform or respond to stimulation. ", and to be a *sluggard* is to be a slothful person, an idler or lazy person."

An idle person will reap nothing but *poverty* and will go hungry; however, the diligent will reap riches (Proverbs 10:4; Proverbs 19:15). According to The American Heritage College Dictionary, poverty is defined in one instance as: "3. Unproductiveness; infertility." *Unproductive* is defined: "1. not productive; idle." On the other hand, *productive* is defined: "2. Producing abundantly; fertile. 3. Yielding favorable or useful results; constructive."; *diligent* is defined: "Earnest, persistent application to an undertaking; assiduity." *Assiduity* is defined: "1. Persistent diligence; unflagging effort." And to be *assiduous* is to be: "1. Constant in application or attention; diligent. 2. Unceasing; persistent."

Now, let's breathe…that was a long one. To sum it up, to be slothful means that you are an idle person accustomed to doing nothing, lazy, you're slow to do what's required, you avoid work or purpose, you're non-productive and infertile (incapable of producing). To be diligent means that you are prosperous, persistent, constant, unceasing in your work, producing abundantly and productive. Remember, spirits operate in the spirit realm like an infection; if you have one symptom you are infected entirely from the root with the entire spirit. Regardless of recognition of all symptoms or spirits in the spirit realm, you must treat the infection from the root because all symptoms are there.

Slothful and Indolence: 1st Period and Period of Delivery

The 1st period in the spirit realm is no different than the 1st trimester that a woman experiences in her pregnancy with regards to the need for you and your body having to adjust to the changes that are taking place. During this change, the body can go in to shut-down mode. Unfortunately, in the spirit realm a very common symptom in the first period is slothfulness and indolence which results in fatigue, frustration, or distraction. Thereby causing you to be disinclined to exert yourself; yielding you no good fruit and can unnecessarily prolong your spiritual pregnancy. If you allow this spiritual infection of Slothfulness to reign in your life, it will definitely rob you of what God has intended for you in this life!

The Period of Delivery is another period that the spirit of Slothfulness is very common and again parallel to the experience of natural pregnancy. After you've been through a lot to get to this period, it is normal to feel as though you can't move forward another inch. You may be tired spiritually and physically during some spiritual pregnancies by the time you get to the brink of your delivery.

In the natural, it is easy for a woman to carry it through to the end due to its tangible nature. In the spirit realm it can be more difficult because often times, you don't know exactly when your breakthrough is coming. More than likely you thought it was a long time ago. Therefore, it is at this intangible point when the enemy will try to slow you down in your process and productivity. Where you once had an over-load of zeal and energy, you may become more lethargic, feeling as though you deserve the rest and the time, because you've been working so hard. Guess what? I've got news for you…start praising God (pushing), because you're almost to the end. You must believe God for strength and endurance and stay the course! Stay up if you must; whatever you must do, go that extra mile! Exert yourself at all cost! Additionally, remember, the JOY of the Lord is your strength (Nehemiah 8:10).

Laziness: 2nd Period

I can't stress how important it is to pay close attention to this symptom in the spirit realm so that you are not robbed of attaining your *True Purpose* in life. Can we address laziness? In the 2nd period of your pregnancy, when you are required to hear from the Holy Spirit regarding your process of implementation, often times, you will be instructed by the Holy Spirit to rise early. Let's just say, He's got to get to you before the world does (the distractions, the calls, the family, the friends, the business….).

> …you've been through a lot to get to this period, it is normal to feel as though you can't move forward another inch.

It is very easy to get caught up in your own agenda without consulting the Holy Spirit. Before you realize it, the day is gone and you have no idea what you've done or if you were productive. Therefore, it will be necessary for you to spend time with Him early or late (whenever your day begins).

In this period your desire to sleep may become greater and at times overwhelming. Maybe even the desire to do absolutely nothing. Nevertheless, it is important that you are quick to obey God. You may not be as responsive in the beginning as you desire to be, but you will get better the closer you get to the delivery of your spiritual birth.

At various points in your spiritual pregnancy, you will be required to exert (strenuous effort) yourself. Just the same, God will require for you to rest in Him in the Spirit as well as in the physical so that you may produce abundantly. This expectation is nothing more than the efforts required for obtaining a college degree or preparing for a test or project. God needs you productive and fertile so that you may produce the *True Purpose* God has for you and through your fulfillment, others will do the same.

How to destroy the spirit of Slothfulness and every branch on its tree:

According to Matthew 16:19:

> *Verily, I say unto you, whatsoever ye shall bind on earth shall be bound in heaven: and whatsoever ye shall loose on earth shall be loosed in heaven.*

Bind: Slothfulness (e.g., the infection)
Loose: Diligence and Productivity (e.g., antibiotic)

The warfare prayer: (Instruction of how to take the antibiotic.)

> *According to Matthew 16:19, I bind up the spirit of Slothfulness and every spirit that comes with the spirit of Slothfulness: Laziness, Poverty, Idleness, Sluggish, and Slothful. In the Name of Jesus, I bind up the spirit of Slothfulness from the root, according to the authority that God has given me in His word and I loose according Proverbs 12:24; 27, a Diligent and Productive spirit!*

Spirit of Slothfulness, you are not welcomed in my life! Slothfulness, I bind you and your entourage up and I cast all into the abyss, prohibiting you to ever return! No weapon formed against me shall prosper as God assures me in (Isaiah 54:17)! No Weapon! This I pray in the Name of Jesus!

NOTE: It is also great to pray in the spirit at this point. Additionally, I would write the definitions of the following words: productive, assiduous and, diligent on individual 3x5 note cards and confess these properties as a part of your life daily.

Now begin to worship God, for He is Almighty and worthy to be praised. Praise Him for the Victory! Praise Him that you are completely guided by the Holy Spirit and nothing or anything has control over your temple of God! Praise God that you are diligent and productive! Praise Him for His promised Word, in which He says that His word will not return unto Him void (Isaiah 55:11)!

THE GOOD SYMPTOMS

No need for a spiritual antibiotic! These are the great symptoms that you will enjoy and be excited to experience!

1. **Joy:** Nehemiah 8:10; Psalm 28:7, 84:5
2. **Perseverance:** Ephesians 6:18; Colossians 1:11
3. **Strong Faith and Love:** Romans 4:20; Luke 16:10;
   Matthew 25:23; Acts 3:16;
   (love and kindness have I drawn thee)
4. **Confidence:** Philippians 3:3-4, II Corinthians 3:11-12
5. **Courage:** I Chronicles 17:25-27, 19:13, 22:13;
   2 Chronicles 32:7; Ezekiel 22:14
6. **Humble Nature:** II Chronicles 34:27; Psalm 25:9
7. **Peace:** Romans 15:13; I Corinthians 14:33

When are these good symptoms most like likely to appear the strongest during your spiritual pregnancy?

1. **Joy:** Transition between 1st Period and 2nd Period,
   Delivery and Manifestation
2. **Perseverance:** 2nd Period, Period of Delivery
3. **Strong Faith and Love:** 2nd Period, 1st Phase of
   Delivery, After Birth, Manifestation
4. **Confidence:** Delivery, Manifestation
5. **Courage:** 2nd Period, Delivery, Manifestation
6. **Humbleness:** Transition between 1st and
   2nd Period, Manifestation
7. **Peace:** 2nd Period to Manifestation

NOTE: Although there are periods specified, understand that you will experience evidence of these positive spirits (symptoms) throughout your spiritual pregnancy. Listed for your reference are the periods in which there most commonly noticed. It may vary from pregnancy to pregnancy and person to person.

Joy
(Transition between 1st Period and 2nd Period, Delivery, Manifestation)

Transition between 1st Period and 2nd Period

In the spirit realm, during the transition between 1st period (pruning) and 2nd period (instruction and direction), you receive clarity of the direction you are headed. Therefore, you are very excited. By this point, you've gone through a lot and you've finally let go of what you were fiercely holding on to!

It is much different than in the natural when a woman can feel and see the baby growing inside of her; as opposed to this blind, foggy experience that you many times can not describe what is taking place. What do you hold on to? How do you maintain your strength to maintain your stand? So it may be a little more difficult at times to find joy in the initial stages of this transition because there's so much you just don't understand. When you begin to receive a clearer direction of where you're going, you get really happy and there may be a sigh of relief, "I'm not crazy after all!" "Yeah!" You also feel some joy for getting passed that 1st period (maybe not knowing that it is only just begun).

The same joy occurs for many women during natural pregnancy. Around a few weeks into the second period, many women are very happy and full of joy because there is no more suffering from morning sickness or hyperemesis (a more severe case of morning sickness – usually lasting all day for sometimes weeks at a time). This sickness or hurt endured by the woman is a result of her body adjusting to the hormonal changes due to pregnancy. As you endure whatever is necessary through the period of conception, in the 1st period and sometimes part of the second period, you may endure some hurt that will eventually bring you to joy and happiness that you can only derive through the spiritual awareness of direction given to you by God.

Delivery

There are several phases within the period of delivery. During the beginning phase of delivery you can really see the light. Your vision is truly nearing the point of manifestation. So close you can taste it! However, depending on the pregnancy you may have more time than you want to acknowledge or realize. Although, the joy and praise that comes over you as you near the end of the tunnel, maintain your faith and stay strong in the word as you ride the course of delivery. It is a beautiful thing to see the light!

Manifestation

What a great sunny day! You have finally delivered the gift that God promised! Oh what joy! Nothing can describe the joy that will come over you at the time of manifestation. You are so full of so many emotions. Quite frankly, words can't describe the joy that feels your heart along with the feeling of accomplishment, humbleness, and thankfulness to God, for He has truly shown Himself to be faithful in your life. Congratulations!

Perseverance: Transition between 2nd and 3rd Period, Period of Delivery and Labor

Transition between 2nd and 3rd Period

According to The American Heritage College Dictionary, persevere (the root of perseverance) is defined: "2. To persist in purpose, an idea, or a task in the face of obstacles or discouragement." During the 2nd Period, you'll be listening and following instruction regarding your purpose. After what you would have more than likely experienced from the periods of Conception, 1st Period and part of 2nd Period, you will definitely persist towards the purpose or direction that you feel the Holy Spirit is leading you. However, it will not be as much of a challenge for you to persevere in the 2nd and 3rd Period as it will be in the period of Delivery.

Period of Delivery

In the period of delivery, although there are moments of excitement, it is no doubt the period that you will endure the greatest challenges of slothfulness, haughtiness, doubt, fear, and unbelief, etc. Nevertheless, in spite of it all, you will persevere! You will press towards the mark of the high call regardless of the distractions that you most likely will face as you near the end of your journey!

Strong Faith (Love), Confidence, Courage, Peace:
Transition between 2nd and 3rd Period, 1st Phase of Delivery, Manifestation

Transition between 2nd and 3rd Period – 1st Phase of Delivery

As a result of the obedience to following God's plan for your life, you will receive this strong faith, confidence, courage, and peace. By the 3rd Period, you have overcome many obstacles and your faith has been tried a few times, to say the least. By the 3rd Period you are sure what God has called you for, so you have strong faith that it is all coming to fruition, you're excited for the mission, and you have the boldness and courage to conquer just about anything to complete God's work through you. By this time, no one can tell you that what you've believed God for will not come to past, and you've definitely paid the price to believe that all things are possible regardless of what it looks like.

1st Phase of Delivery

I must specify the 1st Phase of Delivery is that time that you will feel "strong faith" and indicate that I am not referring to the entire Period of Delivery. As you near the brink of your spiritual delivery, you may not feel as though you have much faith at times due to the attacks from the enemy to try your faith. However, keep the faith and know that what God has promised you WILL come to pass!

Manifestation

You have now delivered what God promised you! Everything that you've gone through is all unbelievable to you. Regardless of your hard work, you realize that what has been birthed through you was NOTHING but God! By the time you reach the point of manifestation, I'll just say, "you couldn't have believed it any better if you had not gone through this process yourself." Your faith is on an entirely different level at this point because the impossible has been made possible through you every step of the way!

Humbleness: Transition between 1st and 2nd Period, Manifestation

Transition between 1st and 2nd Period

As you've already read, in the 1st Period God is pruning you as He prepares you for this spiritual birthing process. You have probably lost some things that you thought were very precious to you, transitioned to a place you never thought you'd be, divorced, ended a relationship, or just as a result of you seeing the work of God in your life to this point, you are most humbled. By the end of the 1st Period, you are most likely more humble than you've ever been in your life! It is amazing what we must go through to get whipped into shape for the call; but, it is OK (II Chronicles 32:7; Ezekiel 22:14).

About the 3rd Period

You may wonder why I failed to mention the 3rd period. In the 3rd period, there are a lot of things you may feel, but for many, humbleness is not felt as strong in this period as in other periods during your spiritual pregnancy. For example, you are really beginning to vision yourself where God said that you would be. You've accomplished things that you never thought would be possible and you also see the light at the end of the tunnel. For many, that light at the end of the tunnel is going to put you in a realm naturally that you never thought you could be. Thereby, the spirit of Haughtiness will present itself more in this period, and many of you will need to remind yourself that it is not you, but God constantly, just to keep yourself grounded.

> You've accomplished things that you never thought you would and you also see the light at the end of the tunnel.

Manifestation

Recognize that as a result of the profound nature of this process that has just been birthed through you, there is no way that you can not give all of the glory to God and be humble when receiving praise for what you've accomplished. "Humble" before God is an understatement of what you will be by the end of this spiritual process. However, be mindful that the enemy will still attempt to destroy that humble nature within you because he understands that a prideful person will be destroyed (Proverbs 16:18). Stay humble and remember, "It is not you; but the God in you that has accomplished this work through you!"

~⚬⚬⚬

CHAPTER 7

The Periods & Phases Of Spiritual Pregnancy

Your road map to a life of Total Fulfillment

I. **Conception - Spiritual Reproduction**
(e.g., Conception)
- How does the process begin?
- How do you know you're on the right track to your destiny?

II. **1st Period - God is Pruning You!**
(e.g., 1st Trimester)

III. **2nd Period — Listening and Following Instructions**
(e.g., 2nd Trimester)

IV. **3rd Period — Delivery Process**
(e.g., Prepping for Labor)
- Planning and Development
- Prepping for Labor

V. **4th Period — Labor and Manifestation**
- Phase I of Early Spiritual Labor
- Phase II of Active Spiritual Labor
- Phase III of Transitional Spiritual Labor
- The Manifestation (e.g., a newborn child)

VI. **Phases of Spiritual Pregnancy**

The Periods & Phases Of Spiritual Pregnancy
(Your road map to a life of Total Fulfillment)

Conception - Spiritual Reproduction (e.g., conception):
The act or process of *True Purpose* being initiated in your life.

How does this process begin?

Have you ever asked the question, "Why am I here?" Regardless if you feel that you are on the right track or not, you need to make a conscious effort towards *True Purpose* in your life. Spiritual Conception may be initiated consciously or unconsciously. A good sign of spiritual conception is when you find yourself being driven to a point in your life where you are completely out of control. Your desires are starting to change or your circumstances have brought you in quest of some answers. However spiritual conception is initiated, you must be sure that you are moving towards *God's Plan*, not *Man's Plan*. Once you have officially made that step towards God's Plan - the *True Purpose* for your life, you have officially spiritually conceived. The goal and often challenge is to make it through the spiritual pregnancy process and keep the faith as God leads you to your final destiny. God only knows what you must experience to get there.

It is possible to be willing or have already committed to follow "God's Plan" for your life and not immediately go into the spiritual pregnancy process which begins in the 1st Period of spiritual pregnancy. The good news is that, as a result of your willingness to go after "God's Plan," you've started the spiritual reproduction process. However, you may experience several spiritual pregnancies before reaching your destiny. As you climax, each spiritual pregnancy will bring about significant change in your life. The evidence of significant change is a great sign that you are entering the first period of a spiritual pregnancy. Keep in mind: you may experience several spiritual pregnancies before reaching your destiny.

> As you climax, each spiritual pregnancy will bring about significant change in your life.

How do you know that you are on the right path?

It is not that easy some times...

Many of you may have been snatched from a position and forced to listen to God while every door was shut as you attempted to open it. Even for me, I look at people that just move or quit a job because God said so, knowing that God will provide for them as He promised in His word. I'd love to be just like Mary, myself. Mary didn't think about all of the possible things that could happen to her before she just said yes (Luke 1:45). Well, in both cases that I experienced significant change or transition I had to get snatched or get to the point that I couldn't do anything else but listen.

As for the current spiritual pregnancy of <u>Pregnant in the Spirit,</u> I was forced to my knees asking God for direction and asking for Him to just tell me before He snatched something else from me. Well, needless to say, it was not that easy! I cried and cried as I felt everything being pulled away and then I asked, "God! Just tell me, please!" I promised Him that I would just try my hardest to move when He instructed me to do so, regardless of the sacrifices on my part. It was then, at my breaking point that God led me to Proverbs 16:3: "Roll your works upon the Lord [commit and trust them wholly to Him; He will cause your thoughts to become agreeable to His will, and] so shall your plans be established and succeed".

Wow! If I roll my works (my cares) over to Him, He will cause my thoughts to become agreeable to His "will", and my plans will be "established and succeed!" So I prayed this prayer, "Lord, I roll all of my cares over to you as you've said in Proverbs 16:3, so, Lord, please make your desires become strongly mine." Once I prayed this prayer, there was such a peace that came over me. I had prayed according to the Word of God and immediately I felt that whatever I was led to do from that point would be the desires of God for me. This is when I received such a peace that passed all understanding (Proverbs 4:7). I knew that God's Word would not return unto Him void (Isaiah 55:11). Once you pray this prayer, you're no longer in control of the driver's seat.

After that Proverbs 16:3 prayer, I began to see the confirmation of God's Word to me. He recalled things He had told me many years ago regarding my purpose. I then began to realize why things went the way they did years ago. Understand, for the call you're required to take certain routes so that you can be a living testimony just as Jesus was. As for me, I continued to Praise God as I continued to go through the course that God had designated for me. Sometimes it wasn't pretty, but it felt a lot better knowing that I had given it to God and I admonish you to do the same. I'm almost certain that you've heard the saying, "It cost to be the boss". Well I believe in the spirit realm, the higher the calling the greater the sacrifice – believe me! OK, you don't have to believe me, but believe God that what I say is true!

Pray this Prayer:

Father, according to Proverbs 16:3, You said that if I roll my works over to You that You will make your desires become mine and so shall my plans be established and succeed. Father, I know that according to Isaiah 55:11, Your Word will not return void to You. I know that as I stand on Your Word, You will honor my prayer. So according to Proverbs 16:3, I roll the purpose for my life over to You and I pray that Your desires become mine so that my plans will be established and succeed. Father, whatever You will that I do, I will say "Yes" to Your will and Your way! So, I thank You for the revelation of Your call in my life and as You lead me I will follow. Cover me in the blood of Jesus Christ. I now step into complete obedience to Your will for my life, my True Purpose. I receive and thank You for the manifestation of Your will in my life today. According to Acts 3:16, I pray this in Jesus' name!

He snatched something else from me. Well, needless to say, it was not that easy! I cried and cried as I felt everything being pulled away and then I asked, "God! Just tell me, please!" I promised Him that I would just try my hardest to move when He instructed me to do so, regardless of the sacrifices on my part.

NOTE: For those that have children, pray, "Father, please reveal to me the purpose for my children so that I may help usher them in the direction you would have them to go, just as Mary and Joseph did for Jesus." If they are of age to talk, you should have them to also pray this prayer. It is OK that the enemy doesn't have any age barriers on whomever he attacks, so you should also prepare your child with that in mind.

The 1st Period - God is Pruning You!
(e.g., 1st Trimester)

In the natural pregnancy process, the 1st trimester can be very difficult for many women. As the body adjusts to all of the hormonal changes due to the pregnancy, a woman may become physically ill. As I've indicated before, a woman often times experiences hyperemesis, extreme fatigue, emotional changes, etc. The symptoms brought on by the hormonal changes to the body may vary from woman to woman, but it is more common than not.

In the spiritual pregnancy process, God's pruning you to further prepare you for the spiritual birthing process, and this is often times, not pleasurable to the flesh. The pruning period can be one of the most difficult periods in the pregnancy. Why? In the process of God putting order in your life for His purpose to be birthed through you, it may be required that God removes things from your life. This may even mean what or whom you feel God put in your life (job, house, car, people, relationships (married or unmarried), career, etc. Although some things He may have put in your life, understand clearly that the season may be over for that particular thing or circumstance. Therefore, you must let go so that God can take you to the next level, or move you to whatever phase necessary for the preparation of spiritual pregnancy. Get ready to say "YES" - "Whatever you want Lord, whatever!" How about some spiritual pre-natal vitamins to ward off whatever spiritual pregnancy symptoms you may be having (the spiritual infections)?

Don't be afraid to put your blind fold on and to move forward in whatever direction God will send you. Jesus came so that you may have life and have it more abundantly (John 10:10). It's important for you to understand that obedience will bring you nothing but blessings. In Deuteronomy 28:11-13, the obedient were promised significant abundance in every area of their lives. Jesus had not yet died for their sins, therefore they were not in right standing with God and the laws were different in that time as opposed to the requirements for the children of God today. You need no mediator (e.g., Moses, Priest, or Preacher) and you are in right standing with God (Romans 10:4). How much more meaning does this passage have to you now that you are in right relationship and with the understanding of the power of the Holy Spirit in your life?

Deuteronomy 28:11-13 – Amplified Version:

And the Lord shall make you have a surplus of prosperity, through the fruit of your body, of your livestock, and of your ground, in the land which the Lord swore to your fathers to give you. The Lord shall open to you His good treasury, the heavens, to give the rain of your land in its season and to bless all the work of your hands; and you shall lend to many nations, but you shall not borrow. And the Lord shall make you the head, and not the tail; and you shall be above only, and you shall not be beneath, if you heed the commandments of the Lord your God which I command you this day and are watchful to do them.

I love this verse of scripture! It is awesome and very simply put. If you follow the commands and be watchful to do them, you will always come out on top! I also love how <u>The Extreme Teen,</u> New Century Version Holy Bible translates this passage...

The Lord will grant you abundant prosperity—(and He Repeats – Glory to God!) in the fruit of your womb, the young of your livestock and the crops of your ground—in the land he swore to your forefathers to give you. The Lord will open the heavens, the storehouse of His bounty, to send rain on your land in season and to bless all the work of your hands. You will lend to many nations but will borrow from none. The Lord will make you the head, not the tail.

If you pay attention to the commands of the Lord your God that I give you this day and carefully follow them, you will always be at the top, NEVER AT THE BOTTOM!

There are many risks that you take in life and many times they don't fair. However, God promises that if you carefully follow His plans, you will "ALWAYS" come out on top, and "NEVER" at the bottom! How wonderful is that? Therefore, in God you have nothing to lose. So you say, "I know how easy you make that sound Princess-O'dilia, but it is not that easy." I understand exactly what you may go through because I'm not oblivious to the challenges one may face with the acceptance of change, particularly challenges faced as a result of this intangible process. Understand that saying yes doesn't mean that you're sure of the direction, nor the plan. "Yes" simply means that you're willing to travel whatever course God has for you while being guided by the Holy Spirit in an effort to accomplish the perfect plan – God's plan for your life – your *True Purpose* – your life of total fulfillment.

2nd Period - Listening and Following Instructions
(e.g., 2nd Trimester)

The second period is very similar to the second trimester of a woman's pregnancy. In the natural, most women experience relief of the changes they possibly endured in the 1st trimester as their body adjusted to the hormonal changes occurring as a result of the pregnancy. I know for me, I was relaxed, excited, and I wanted to start working on the room for the baby. I was no longer extremely fatigue, I could eat what I wanted, I could exercise, etc.

In the spirit realm, the second period is also the lighter; the more relaxed of the periods. Now that you've said "YES" to *True Purpose* and have mentally transitioned, God will begin to reveal to you what you are having in the spirit realm. Yes, you can relax a little now, but in God's presence constantly! **DO NOT** move ahead of God! To step ahead of God's instruction may cause for a miscarriage or even a spiritual abortion of the call as a result of you following your own understanding and becoming frustrated when it doesn't turn out like you thought. I know it is exciting to finally have a pretty good idea of where you're headed, but **FOLLOW GOD!** You don't know as much as you think you know. Remember: God is teaching you to trust Him solely (not mans process or plan, but His) and God's process does not always make common sense, but it is revelation sense obtained under the power of the Holy Spirit!

Additionally, in this period, you must prepare for great battle in the spirit realm and learn the opposing side, as you read in Chapter 7. I can't stress enough the importance of you learning of the opposing side (the nature and opposition of your flesh).

Consider a sports game: To win a championship, you learn the strong points about the other team, especially the key players so that you can set up defense against them. How else can you win victoriously if you have no knowledge of the opposing side? You can't. The spirit realm is NO DIFFERENT! Although you will be attacked by many spirits, there are some key players on the field that will step forward when you are implementing *True Purpose* in your life that may not otherwise be prevalent. Knowledge is power and you must apply the knowledge that you obtain regarding the spirit realm to your life in order to accomplish this process required for fulfillment. Understand how to battle spirit realm properly. You must be geared up because the enemy and his entourage will definitely turn it up a few dials in the 3rd Period.

Therefore put on God's complete armor, that you may be able to resist and stand your ground on the evil day [of danger], and, having done all [the crisis demands], to stand [firmly in your place]. (Ephesians 10:13—Amplified Version)

3rd Period - Delivery Process
(e.g., prepping for Labor)

The third period is very mixed. You've gained a lot more confidence and have learned to trust in God a lot more. In this period, the enemy will attack your confidence and faith on everything that you've believed throughout your entire pregnancy. Remember, this is not a tangible experience; all you have is your faith. "God, did I hear you right?" perhaps will cross your mind. Remember, the last thing the enemy wants is for you to deliver! As a result, you may wander back and forth between joy and excitement and feelings caused by the attacks from the enemy, which will come very strong; for example, Depression, Deception, Seducing Spirits, Doubt, Fear, Unbelief...Regardless of whatever obstacle you face, if you fall down, GET BACK UP AND DELIVER THE PURPOSE THAT GOD HAS SPECIFICALLY CALLED FOR YOU TO DELIVER!

Remember this: God knew what you were going to do and what you would be faced with before you were conceived with this purpose! In the natural, the woman is instructed to PUSH, in the spirit realm you are instructed to PRAISE! PRAISE! PRAISE! **PRAISE *TRUE PURPOSE* INTO ACTIVE POSITION IN YOUR LIFE!**

What you should expect in delivery

In the natural, an expectant woman can experience the delivery process for a long period of time. A prime example: I was in labor with my son for two days and I pushed for three and a half hours! Although this may not be the story for many women, this was my experience delivering my first child. As for my second child, my daughter, it was different. My daughter was delivered within a day and I gave her about three or four good pushes and she was out. For both of my children, when it was time for me to go to the hospital, I didn't experience the traditional signs the doctor said that I would. Nonetheless, with some signs being visible, I knew that it was time for me to go. In spiritual delivery, you may be at the point of "delivery" for a while before it is time for you to actually deliver what God has promised you.

Some pregnancies are more difficult than others. Like the ole cliché goes, "The bigger you are, the harder you fall." Well in life and I believe especially for this spiritual birthing process, the bigger the call or responsibility, the harder the battle. During the 1st and 2nd periods you were challenged, but consider those periods as the conditioning periods for the final period. By this time you've been whipped and have gone through some experiences that you'd rather not had gone through, but yet you continued on with what God has called for you to do (I commend you). You're also thoroughly convinced that you are definitely in the will of God and you just want to complete the task that God has given to you.

The feelings that you may experience are very similar to what an expectant mother may feel during a natural pregnancy. "OK, I've been carrying this baby for 7 – 8 months and I've been to 10+ office visits. I'm ready to be trained on how to push this baby out!" In spite of the anxious feelings of delivery, she also prepares for the baby shower because she knows there is a slim chance for a miscarriage. At this point, there is no looking back. The baby is coming, rather she likes it or not!

By this time, even if there has been extreme difficulty during the pregnancy, the faith that this baby is going to be born is simply a reality in the expectant mother's mind. The doctor could tell her their going to need to take the baby via a cesarean due to complications or they may even inform her that they foresee there being some challenges during the delivery. In spite of any negative news the woman may receive, I can almost guarantee you that the expectant mother will continue in faith that her baby is coming. The baby shower will take place, as well as any other plans. Even if at times the enemy should come to her with doubt that her baby will not make it, I'm sure most women would push those feelings of doubt to the side.

Well that's just fine, because in the natural you act on faith sometimes without too much effort. At the end of the day the enemy knows that it is easier for a woman to plan for a natural delivery due to its tangible nature as opposed to you having faith in this intangible process. For that matter, a woman's faith is more grounded and consistent throughout the entire pregnancy process. In the spirit realm it is intangible and the enemy knows that he has a better chance of distracting you with opposition because you'll have no knowledge of where the distractions are derived. He realizes that without knowledge of this intangible process to fulfillment (spiritual pregnancy), you're most likely to abort the process than to deliver. It is also very likely for you to assume that your choice to spiritually abort was a divine choice due to the opposition.

This period is when the spirit of slothfulness will also present itself more (and you thought the first period was bad). The closer you near those final moments, for many people slothfulness will go to another level of challenge. Not because you wish to be slothful, but you are tired of carrying this spiritual gift. It is also no different than in the natural for a woman. The closer a woman gets to the end and her belly gets bigger and bigger, she gets a little tired of carrying that load. She wants the baby out at all cost and it gets a little more difficult to move around as she once did in the beginning periods of her spiritual pregnancy.

So, in this phase you must understand that there are many spirits (via, through a person or in the spirit realm) that will come to challenge you in an attempt to have you abort even at this late stage in your spiritual pregnancy. I'll use Peter as an example: Peter who walked on water for a while by faith, at the end of his stretch, realized what "he" had done and began to sink (Matthew 14:30-31). I'm sure Peter suddenly thought about what "he" was not capable of. He began to sink because He completely lost sight of God. Why? The spirit of doubt came all over him (Matthew 14:31). He let down his shield of faith. Oh, but God always has a ram in the bush! Jesus reached out to Peter, so that he would not fall, and Peter made it to the end of that stretch. God is so AWESOME!

The enemy knows that you are almost there. His objective is to deter your faith and to distract you so that you will lose sight of God. In other words, distract you from the TRUTH that *only through the power of God are you capable to do the impossible* (Philippians 4:13; Colossians 3:16)! He will challenge you with doubt, fear, and unbelief. He also will begin to distract you with life's circumstances, family, career, finances, etc. He will do anything to keep you from completing the work of God that is operating through you.

> The enemy knows that you are almost there. His objective is to deter your faith and to distract you so that you will lose sight of God.

Again, I can't stress this point enough. "Regardless of whatever the enemy challenges you with at this point, know that it is not you that is doing the work, it is through the power of God that through you the impossible is being made possible." As a result of God's power in you, ALL things are possible! Recall what you read in Chapter 3 about Mary and how the impossible was fulfilled through her as a result of her faith. Know that you are called for greatness and its God's power in you that will cause you to make it through this period. Again, it is not you, but God's Power in you for His Glory! Amen.

Preparing for Labor

At this point, you've gotten your plans and you've been completing tasks and getting in position for delivery as you persevered through the 2nd period. You may feel as if you're ready to deliver at any time, so you must be very careful to pace yourself. You should be very excited by now because you've gotten a lot in order for the delivery of what God has promised. Wow! This is getting very close to home and you're starting to experience moments where you are so excited, you're smiling because the vision is so clear to you and you're feeling a little pressure. You feel as though you can almost touch what you've been waiting for. However, you've got more to do before you get there.

Spiritual Braxton Hicks

This pressure that you will experience from both ends is called Spiritual Braxton Hicks. In the natural pregnancy process, Braxton Hicks are the irregular contractions that an expectant mother experiences as the uterus is tightening up as it gears the body for the big day. These irregular contractions feel like moments of strong pressure that may cause a little discomfort to the woman. She's instructed to breathe through the moments of pressure. In comparison to the true contractions that she experiences during transitional labor (the final phase), Braxton Hicks are very mild. Although the pressure doesn't subside, the breathing causes her to relax as she endures the moment of pressure. Believe it or not,

Spiritual Braxton Hicks are very similar. As you begin to position yourself for the big day, you feel pressure at times, or I'll just say overwhelmed and excited at the same time. However, it comes over you like a wind, suddenly and unexpected. Just breathe and continue praising as you continue moving towards the big day of manifestation. It is not time.

4th Period - Labor and Manifestation
(e.g., Labor and the Birth of a New Born Child)

- **Phase I – Early Spiritual Labor**
  (e.g., Early Labor-Phase I)

- **Phase II – Active Spiritual Labor**
  (e.g., Active Labor-Phase II)

- **Phase III - Transitional Spiritual Labor**
  (e.g., Transitional Labor – Phase III)

- **Manifestation**
  (e.g., Birth of a New Born Child)

Phase I - Early Spiritual Labor
(Early Labor – Phase I)

Although this period is not very long verses the duration of the entire pregnancy in the natural, nor in the spiritual, it is the toughest period to get through for both scenarios. In the spirit realm, you're like the woman in the period of Labor when her contractions are about 5 minutes apart, her water has broken, and her cervix is dilating more progressively (some women [e.g., my experience] actually began to dilate during the experiences of the Braxton Hicks, maybe for about 1 or 2 centimeters of the 10 needed before the expectant mother is considered to be in labor). It is now time to rush her to the hospital. In the spirit realm you are experiencing more pressure at an increased level of intensity than what you've already experienced through this entire intangible process.

The combined feelings of being overwhelmed and excited will become even more intense in this period. Additionally, the enemy will really attempt to distract you. More than likely you're feeling like you have the faith that could literally move mountains, but you are ready to deliver and it doesn't seem to be coming fast enough! You're at the point that it is time for you to deliver the spiritual gift; however, as a result of the demands on you at this time, you may be struggling to continue riding the course with God. As a matter of fact, you may often ask God, "Can this be done? Please!" Keep riding. You will deliver when it is His time.

Phase II - Active Spiritual Labor
(Active Labor-Phase II)

Active Labor is the period that you will be really attacked by the enemy, and of course, the enemy does not like that you're almost to the point of manifestation. I also believe that some things that you experience are tests from God to make you stronger and for you to also realize how far you've come with your faith. You've got the pressure coming from both ends. Consequently, you're right in the place you need to be for everything to be as it was planned before your existence!

Again, think about everything Jesus went through in the garden of Gethsemane (Matthew 26). Jesus' ministry was nearing completion here on earth and now it was time for Jesus to cross the road that would lead Him to His destiny. He was already dealing with the emotions of fear and depression. In addition, He had friends betraying Him, friends falling short when He needed them the most, and at such a time, He couldn't get a response from God and He felt abandoned. Wow! Yet in love, He remained until His death and His words even as He took His last breathe was, *"Father, forgive them for they know not what they do."* (Luke 23:34) Jesus did not judge the people for their actions; rather He prayed for their forgiveness. Thereby, you are to be as Jesus was and recognize that although you will face opposition that may also come through people, you must stay the course in love and without judgment.

At this point, it seems that before you can recover from putting out one fire you're putting out another fire in your life. Realistically, you may feel at times that you can't make it to the next level if one more situation or an obstacle comes, seemingly, to get you off your path to *True Purpose.* However, you are much stronger than you may realize, to deal with what you are dealing with as a result of everything that you have foregone in this spiritual pregnancy. What do you do? You must breathe in the Spirit, which means to PRAISE! You must give Praise and Glory to God for His goodness and for what you are birthing into your life! Give thanks for everything that you've gone through and how this spiritual process has impacted your life (Psalm 105:1)! Remember, the joy of the Lord is your strength (Nehemiah 8:10) and no weapon formed against you shall prosper (Isaiah 54:17).

Phase III - Transitional Spiritual Labor
(Transitional Labor – The Final Phase)

You're almost at the finish line. In the natural, this phase is when the expectant mother has gone through all of her labor and now her cervix has dilated from 1 cm to 10 cm, which means the baby is in position to come out. For the baby to be delivered, the mom must now get in position to push the baby out. In this process, the doctor wants the woman to push when the contraction comes;

so, right at the time of the pain, she is to push. In the Spirit Realm, you are to PRAISE every time you feel the pressure from wherever or whomever. PRAISE and WORSHIP (giving God the highest THANKS) your way into manifestation!

Spiritual Epidural

I remember when I was pregnant with my son I was given an epidural so that I could endure the labor "with minimal or no pain". When it was time for me to push, after a few pushes the doctor told the nurse to turn the epidural off because she felt that I needed to feel more pain in order to push properly.

Some of you may feel as though you've been at the point of manifestation for a long time and it is just not coming forth. You're thinking that you can use a spiritual epidural at anytime now. You may feel as if things don't come through really soon, you may not make it. In the spirit realm, your spiritual epidural is the joy of the Lord! This supernatural joy will give you that ability to rest and not feel the effects of the situations around you as much as you would if you did not have the joy of the Lord.

Are you ready for the manifestation?

At the time the doctor turned off the epidural, the pain became suddenly more than I thought I would possibly be able to bare. As a result of the duration of time that I was in labor and the pain that I endured in spite of the epidural, I prayed to God because I didn't think I could continue through to delivery. I proceeded to let "God" know that I was going to give up. Well it wasn't my time so a bright idea came to mind, I believe by the Holy Spirit. I had decided that the next time the doctor told me to stop pushing when the contraction stopped that I was going to keep pushing until the baby came. Otherwise, I had decided that I would die on that table and let the Doctors remove the baby from me. After three and a half hours of pushing and my son not coming, one strong continuous push and he came as the Doctor screamed, "Stop pushing!"

As I had to be persistent in the midst of my pain and greatest feeling of defeat, you must be persistent. In spite of what you're feeling, give your greatest push. As the pressure comes on, begin to give thanks to God for the manifestation of the miracle He is birthing through you! In spite of what you see, PRAISE and give THANKS! How deep is your praise? Remember, thankfulness is most powerful because it is an affirmation that you believe that God has done what He has already promised. It won't be long before you'll see the manifestation sooner than you could ever believe!

Manifestation
(e.g., Delivery of a New Born Child)

Congratulations on your delivery! I'm sure that you can barely believe the spiritual pregnancy is over and you can barely imagine what you had to go through to get here. Now you are to deliver the testimony of this special gift to as many would hear. Use the experience as an opportunity to uplift God through Praise and Worship and acknowledgement of what He's done through you.

Remember everything that you've read here in <u>Pregnant in the Spirit</u> with regards to how the enemy will try to come and interfere on the joy that you feel and the sense of accomplishment that you may have (e.g., the enemy will try to rain on your parade). Even at this point the enemy will come to attack your confidence with doubt, fear, and unbelief in an attempt to prevent you from either giving credit to Whom credit is do or in an attempt to drive you under the subjection of a Haughty Spirit (Proverbs 16:18; 21:24). The enemy knows that a haughty spirit will deter you down a road to destruction. Do not lose site of God and don't allow the enemy to steal your joy nor your gift from you!

PHASES OF SPIRITUAL PREGNANCY

After-Birth
(e.g., loving and appreciating the child God blessed you with)

Yes, the spiritual pregnancy process is over. So now you must nurture what God has birthed through you. Appreciate the replicate of the work of the cross that God has just completed through you! Continue to follow God's instruction through the guidance of the Holy Spirit as you did to successfully reach the point of manifestation. So, rather your delivery was a new house, or a new career, you need to maintain your focus on God. Whatever God has done through you, it is to be handled as a prize possession in a most humble and joyous sense.

Understand that because it is all for the glory of God, you must understand that you are not to make it a god in your life, but know that you must be free with what you've been given in the spirit realm. This means, if the Holy Spirit requires you to give it away at some point, you must do that. If you were blessed with a house, you are to keep it holy and always honor God! For example, if you were blessed with a business, a ministry, or whatever, you are to operate in love and under the control of the Holy Spirit so that God may always get the glory through the work that has been completed through you!

Spiritual Abortion
(e.g., abortion)

Unfortunately, in the natural, a female may abort her child through 6 months of pregnancy. In the spirit realm, it is possible to abort the call of God on your life at anytime during the spiritual pregnancy process and even through manifestation. If you birth the gift and do nothing with what He has completed through you, you have made the choice to abort in the spirit realm.

Can you recover?

Yes! Thank God! The timing for what you have aborted may or may not have passed; however, if you turn to God, He will do an even greater work through you. Remember the prayer of Proverbs 16:3 that you read in Chapter 4.

Spiritual Premature Birth
(e.g., early term pregnancy)

Be very careful: if you are too anxious, you may get tired of the process and although God may be leading you (you're feeling strong in your spirit) to go a step further before you submit your project or speak in a seminar, or open your business, or get married, or buy a house, etc, you decide to move ahead of God. God may have revealed to you what you're going to birth into your life; however, to ensure the victory that was promised, you must stay "His" course!

Result

When you experience spiritual premature birth, you may find yourself very discouraged because the gift will not turn out like God planned. Often times, people completely abort the spiritual pregnancy at this point because they feel they were completely misled down the wrong road or followed the wrong dream because of how things turned out. On the other hand, some people decide to settle, instead of moving forward as God has instructed and experiencing a life of fulfillment.

Spiritual Postpartum Depression
(e.g., postpartum depression)

A great parallel of this would be to a woman that has delivered a child and as a result of postpartum depression she is not able to care for her child. According to the American Heritage College Dictionary, depression is defined: "4…an inability to concentrate, insomnia, and feelings of sadness, dejection, and hopelessness. 5.a. A reduction in activity or force. b. A reduction in physiological vigor or activity. c. A lowering in amount, degree, or position."

I Experienced Spiritual Postpartum Depression

I'll give you an example of a spiritual postpartum depression that I suffered. After my first book The Armor of God was published and released, initially I was so excited for the manifestation of this project. However, after the book was released, I began to over analyze the results of the book and I began to lose confidence in what I had been blessed to accomplish. What was wrong? I suddenly lacked confidence in the final product. I noticed a few things that I would have done differently and assumed that my issue would be the issue of every person that read the book. So, I stopped putting the dedication and time in the project because I had lost faith in what God had done through me.

Ironically enough, every time someone would read the book they would talk about how it guided them spiritually and yielded them so much more confidence in there walk with God and in their daily lives. Each time I heard a testimony I would be reminded of Who inspired me to do that great work. I eventually realized that in God is perfection and in God is the manifestation of all great things. I also eventually realized that I was in no position to make the choice to not continue to take His work to the potential He intended for it to be through me.

When God showed me through my error what Spiritual Postpartum Depression was, He used a parallel between a God's spiritual gift birthed through you and a child that is born with what we call, a "handicap". To not go forth with what God has done through you is like a mother delivering a child into this world with a handicap and as a result of that handicap, the mother decides not to care for that child. In such a case, society would frown on this woman and label her as a heartless misfit-mom.

Regardless of what you view as error, it is yet your responsibility and it is irrelevant to God. The baby is your responsibility to love and nurture just as the spiritual gift that God has spiritually birthed through you is your responsibility to see forth. God's work is all perfect and in God's divine order. I had to realize that God was going to get the glory and that people would interpret the gift as He wished for them to interpret the gift. My job was just to continue in obedience, zeal, and gratitude for the work of God through me! The rest would have been handled by God.

Spirit Realm Assignments
(e.g., twins, triplets or birthing more than one child at different times)

Once the spiritual reproductive process begins, only God knows what will be accomplished through the power of God given to you. Although you may have one ultimate destiny for your life (e.g., to help people, to teach, to be a mom, an attorney, a father, an engineer, President, entrepreneur, to minister), you may have several assignments (several duties) that must be accomplished as you travel the road to your ultimate destiny, the divine level of fulfillment, peace, confidence, freedom, and joy attainable through God. It is also very likely that you may be required to complete a few assignments at once.

An example may be:

Purpose: To build a Homeless Shelter that will house 100s of families and provide food and clothing.

Assignments:

1. Lead a convention to awareness of the growing rate of homeless people
2. Feed the homeless people each week for 2 years at another shelter
3. Open a center for abused women and children
4. Offer assistance to a needy family each month

One assignment may not require you to go through as extensive of a process as it does for another. Nonetheless, for each assignment there will be this spiritual pregnancy process that you must go through. Hence, you may have to say "Yes" a few times. When your desires initially shift to where God has planned for them to shift, from that moment, you may complete several assignments along the way or some assignments in conjunction with another before reaching your destiny.

For example, you may be feeding the homeless people each week at the same time you are building a center for abused women and children. You also may be starting the process of building the homeless shelter for 100s of families at the same time you are assisting families each month and attempting to plan for a major world-wide convention. You may feel that God's destiny for you is in one area, when in fact, God has a much greater plan for you. As a matter of fact, the assignments are designated to prep you for your final destination. That's the mystery of God and it leaves for such a great Manifestation each time!

The Duration of Spiritual Pregnancy

Unlike the natural pregnancy process where there is a specified time for the trimesters and for the duration of the pregnancy, only God knows the specific time in spiritual pregnancy. In natural pregnancy, the Doctors can only tell an expectant mother the approximate time of her due date which is 9 months and maybe even a little longer. The Doctors will only allow for the pregnancy to go so far before they intervene and schedule a delivery date. On this date the doctor will either induce the labor or perform a cesarean section. In the spiritual pregnancy process you should rest in knowing that God will not put on you more than you can handle (Psalm 42:6).

An interesting theory is the time of pregnancy as it relates to spiritual pregnancy. In spiritual pregnancy there is no definite time. Based on the current observations it has been about one year from the time of 1st Period to Manifestation. For instance, although in some pregnancies I was aware of the vision, I may have taken notes or felt as though I was headed in the direction of the spiritual pregnancy process (1st Period), it may have been two years later that I actually began the process.

Based on my current observations, God plants thoughts, ideas, and plans in your mind to prep you for spiritual pregnancy once you have committed to seek God's Plan and not Man's Plan. When it is time for you to start the spiritual pregnancy process for an assignment or your final destiny, there will be significant adjustment in your life as your flesh adjusts to what's getting ready to take place spiritually through you. From the 1st Period to the Period of Manifestation, it has been observed in several cases to be about 1 year if you allow the entire spiritual pregnancy process to take its course.

The Duration of the Spiritual Pregnancy for <u>*Pregnant in the Spirit*</u>

Personally, I realized that I would write this book about 4 years ago. I began to take notes as things would come to mind, and I began to talk about this book that I would write. At that moment, I had no idea of what roads I would have to cross in order for me to even start the spiritual pregnancy process (1st Period). However, from the moment the spiritual pregnancy process began (1st Period) it was about one year just as it was for my first two spiritual pregnancies.

Within the past year, I've experienced a profound message, a profound concept, a new business, a dissolved business, a tremendous purpose and mission, a responsibility to the world, a new outlook on God, some losses, some gains, and a personal breakthrough in the natural as well as in the spiritual. From this, I'll never be the same. To look back over what has happened within this year brings chills up and down my spine. I can't believe all that has occurred.

I must admit, of the three spiritual pregnancies that I've had, this one was the most challenging. I guess because this is where I enter my destiny and I now realize that everything that I've been through was for this moment here.

Transitioning in the Spirit Realm
(e.g., letting go of your children)

Transitioning in the spirit realm can be one of the most difficult experiences of your life. At this point, you are required to let go of what you were sure that God had planned for your life, so that you may graduate to another level of God's plan for you. Most times you may feel at this point that you are comfortable and at peace. To discern that God is taking you to another level is a phenomenon, so you must be Spirit led. Unfortunately, most people don't move easily in this phase. For example, it is not as easy as the tangible process of letting go of your children when they reach a certain age. For many, in the spirit realm, circumstances usually bring an individual to the point of accepting transition; others by strong desire (typically derived by the guidance of the Holy Spirit); and others by knowingly obeying the direction of the Holy Spirit.

CHAPTER 8

WHY NOT ACCEPT JESUS CHRIST?

WHY NOT ACCEPT JESUS CHRIST?

The Leader in the Movement for God

Consider this: Not accepting Jesus Christ and striving for a personal relationship with God (becoming a part of the Christ Movement: the Movement for God and Spiritual Equality) is like being against racial segregation and not signing up on Dr. Martin Luther King's Team for the Movement against segregation and not accepting that God appointed him as the Leader over that Movement.

To accept Jesus Christ is to accept the power of God, the love of God, the ability of God, and the freedom given by God through the sacrifice of the life of Jesus Christ as TRUTH. To accept what God did through the life of Jesus Christ is to accept what He can do through you!

What is the difference between the "begotten Son and the adopted child"?

Jesus Christ is the begotten Son because He is the only child that God took of Himself and through Spirit created a child in the flesh. The rest of us were born of a fleshly union.

Aside this, there is no difference! We are to honor and respect our brother for what He did for us. Jesus carried out His mission and we should honor and respect Him for that great sacrifice and live our lives as an example of our Father as Jesus did! God – the Father of Truth, Love and Freedom wants us never to forget what Jesus did for us. God wants us to accept the power of the Holy Spirit and continue the mission that Jesus started. By this we can also live a life of fulfillment and encourage others to do the same.

Remember, the purpose of the sacrifice was to give us the opportunity of eternal salvation, freedom, love, the possibility of victory in every area of our lives and to demonstrate the love that God has for us! This is why we accept Jesus Christ as our personal Lord and Savior. He is the leader of this mission and He definitely paid the price for that!

Do you accept the mission of Dr. Martin Luther King? Although the sacrifice that he made for the freedom for all was most honorable, it is not eternal! Are you a follower of the dream of Dr. Martin Luther King, Jr.? The dream he had for equality, freedom, love, and peace for all? How many believe that Dr. Martin Luther King, Jr. was guided by the Holy Spirit?

Jesus gave us the opportunity for eternal freedom, love, peace and a life of fulfillment! Jesus spread the message of God! If you believe in God, the Almighty, the Creator, the Omnipotent, the Powerful, the Faithful, the Father of Truth, Love,

> Jesus also operated through the power of God and honored God for all that He did while He was here on earth.

and Freedom, you believe as Jesus did and you are a follower of Jesus Christ. Jesus also operated through the power of God and honored God for all that He did while He was here on earth.

Now why not acknowledge out of your mouth that you believe that Jesus, your spiritual brother came and died for your freedom through the power of God? From this moment, continue to serve and glorify God as Jesus did by attaining a life of fulfillment, your

True Purpose and it will make God so happy.

God wants no division amongst His children...

Not accepting Jesus Christ is like not accepting one of the siblings in your family. To accept Jesus Christ is to accept the power of His existence and the love that He had for us to carry out the purpose for which He was created. His demonstration of lifestyle shows that the "apple doesn't fall too far from the tree" as He demonstrated unconditional love for us. He was a replicate of Father God – our Father just as we should be. Let's all acknowledge Jesus Christ as our most Honorable Brother, our Savior and get to know God, our Father the way He got to know God through the Holy Spirit. God wants unity and that has been demonstrated through the lives of many here on earth as He gave them the courage and ability to sacrifice for the well-being, freedom, and opportunity of others. Can we say "It's a family affair?"

God shows no favoritism

Consider a family who adopted a few children and they had a few children of their own. If the parents of these children decided to treat the adopted children different from the ones that were conceived between their fleshly union, people would consider that to be unfair. One may wonder, "Why did they even adopt the children?"

The adopted parents are expected to love all of the children the same. The parents are expected not to have any favoritism between the children. Yes, the parents will always know that there is a natural bond between the ones birthed, but there should never be a difference in the way the children are treated. How would it be if the parents sent the birthed children to an elite private school and they sent the adopted children to an average public school? Insane? Do you think God is like this parent? Imagine God saying, "I'll work the impossible through Jesus Christ and you all can figure it out for yourselves." Could you imagine God to love or treat His children differently? Not the God I know.

I want you all to see that to not recognize the sacrifice and the power that was demonstrated through the life of Jesus Christ, is to not possibly realize the power and ability that God desires to do in your life. He will not show favoritism between His children! The same love, power and ability God showed through Jesus is in you! How much do you believe?

What is the saying?
DON'T LET THE DREAM DIE!

As we continue to uphold the mission of the late Dr. Martin Luther King, Jr. of freedom and togetherness, as one people for as long as we live in this world. Like so should we uphold the mission of Jesus Christ for spiritual equality, eternal freedom, peace, joy, and fulfillment all attainable through the power of God in you (the Holy Spirit). Let's strive for the "personal relationship" with God.

I believe if Jesus Christ had a dream, it would be that all people would love one another, we'd come together as one, we'd stop judging, there would be no religious bondages, we'd understand that there is NO condemnation, and we'd recognize that it's all about God's plan being accomplished in our lives. Finally, we'd then recognize the true meaning of the Jesus Christ Movement: love and freedom without judgment and condemnation that is provided through the power of the Holy Spirit in our lives!

I love you all!
To be continued…

Appendices

Appendix I
Key Terms

Spiritual Pregnancy (e.g., natural pregnancy): is the process of attaining True Purpose in your life. This intangible process (conception to manifestation) is accomplished only with one's choice of being guided by God's Spirit that is within and one's willingness to be free from the bondages of religion and the traditional processes of man. (See Pages 16, 209-238)

Spiritual Abortion (e.g., abortion): To avoid or stop the spiritual pregnancy process from being active in your life. (See Pages 24, 64, 72, 118, 127, 151, 217, 231)

Spiritual Premature Birth (e.g., early term pregnancy): to move ahead of God in His plan and you deliver before God's timing. (See Page 232)

Spiritual Postpartum Depression (e.g., postpartum depression): to become merely immobilized to move forward with what God has blessed you with after the manifestation for reasons of doubt, fear, unbelief, or lack of confidence. To decide not to nurture or go forth with the miracle that God has given you. (See Pages 233-234)

Spiritual Realm Assignments (e.g., twins, triplets or birthing more than one child at different times): The process of birthing more than one gift under the inspiration of the Holy Spirit simultaneously or not. (See Page 234)

Spiritual Pregnancy Duration (e.g., natural pregnancy term): Based on current study, approximately 1 year from the 1st Period. As the study of this intangible process progresses, the results will be documented. (See Page 236)

Transitioning in the Spirit Realm (e.g., letting go of your children): 1. To go from one level of the call of God to another level of the call of God for your life, (being totally committed to spiritual guidance) 2. To move towards the process of being guided by the Holy Spirit for the purpose of attaining *True Purpose* for your life. 3. To move into your destiny. (See Pages 17, 238)

Spiritual Conception (e.g., conception): 1. The act or process of True Purpose (God's predestined plan) being initiated in your life. 2. The Spiritual Reproduction Process. (See Pages 210-214)

Spiritual Pregnancy Periods: There are four periods: 1st Period (God Pruning); 2nd Period (Listening and following Instruction from God); 3rd Period – Delivery (Planning and Development); 4th Period - Labor and Manisfestation [Three Phases: (1) Early (2) Active (3) Transitional]. Due to the intangible nature of this process and the lack of human control, there can be no definite time determined for each period. (See Pages 210-230)

Spiritual Epidural (e.g., epidural): The Joy and Peace that comes from trusting in God through this process. (See Page 228)

Spiritual Manifestation (e.g., the delivery of a new born child): The completion of the spiritual pregnancy process. To attain *True Purpose* – Total Fulfillment. (See Pages 81,130,229,230)

Spiritual Delivery (e.g., Delivery): The Planning and Development Period of Spiritual Pregnancy. (See Pages 218-224)

Spiritual Braxton Hicks (e.g., Braxton Hicks): The pressure of excitement and turmoil experienced simultaneously. (See Page 223)

Spiritual After-Birth (e.g., loving your child): The act of nurturing the gift that God has given. (See Page 231)

Refer to Appendix II (Spiritual Pregnancy vs. Natural Pregnancy Chart) for a quick reference of Spiritual Pregnancy Terms and Phases.

APPENDIX II

NATURAL PREGNANCY vs. SPIRITUAL PREGNANCY

(Chart)

NATURAL PREGNANCY vs. SPIRITUAL PREGNANCY

~ At a Glance ~

(Applicable to Men and Women)

PERIOD OR PHASE	NATURAL PREGNANCY	SPIRITUAL PREGNANCY
Natural Pregnancy - Natural Conception and Reproduction **Spiritual Pregnancy** - Spiritual Conception and Reproduction	Formation of a viable zygote (cell) by the union of the sperm and the ovum; fertilization (the act or process of "initiating" biological reproduction by insemination or pollination.)	The act or process of True Purpose being initiated in your life. Have you ever asked the question, "Why am I here?" Regardless if you feel that you are on the right track or not, you need to make a conscious effort towards True Purpose in your life. Spiritual Conception may be initiated consciously or unconsciously. A good sign is when you find yourself being driven to a point in your life when you are completely out of control; your desires are starting to change; your circumstances have brought you in quest of some answers... However spiritual conception is initiated, you must be sure that you are moving towards God's Plan, not Man's Plan. Once you have officially made that step towards God's Plan, the True Purpose for your life you have officially spiritually conceived – you have started the spiritual reproduction process.
Natural Pregnancy – 1st Trimester: Months 1 – 3 after conception	• Fertilization and Ovulation	• Spiritual Pregnancy begins

Spiritual Pregnancy – 1st Period: God's pruning you to prep you for the pregnancy (desires, comfort level, job, self, marriage, boyfriend, girlfriend, home, car.....)	• The uniting of the egg and uterus • Evidence of Pregnancy • Body begins to change – hormones are rising • Morning or All Day Sickness occur in many women as a result of the hormonal changes. • Severe Fatigue • Increased appearance of veins: blood supply needed to nourish the growing fetus • Begin taking prenatal vitamins (progesterone) which may cause gas • Dizziness – Signs of increased blood to the baby resulting in lower blood pressure and reduced blood pressure to expectant mother's brain – giving the expectant mother a dizzy feeling.	• God will begin to alter your life, will, and emotions but this may be a tough alteration process. You may feel some pain. • God will begin to prune you of whatever (job, home, relationship, etc.) that may conflict with the delivery of True Purpose in your life (via Assignment to the Purpose or the actual final position that God has planned for you), whatever God needs to alter in your life so that you can have an opportunity to be a light to others as a result of the fulfillment in your life. • You may become overwhelmed with fatigue, slothfulness, procrastination, and even resistance as you experience the changes that you must go through in order to be properly prepared for the spiritual delivery. • Many of you will begin to seek God's word more as you wonder what's going on (much may be unclear in this period) as you fight to hold on to things that God will require you to let go – it's necessary that He strips you of your desire! It's not about you; it's about God's plan for your life!

PERIOD OR PHASE	NATURAL PREGNANCY	SPIRITUAL PREGNANCY
	• Dizziness – Signs of increased blood to the baby resulting in lower blood pressure and reduced blood pressure to expectant mother's brain – giving the expectant mother a dizzy feeling.	• Many may resist the transformation, which generally could result in the loss of what you're trying to hold on to. It's better to just Let Go, but that's not always as easy as it sounds, so, God will gladly remove it from you. • You may have feelings of frustration. " God what do you want from me?! • Once you've Let Go, God snatched, or you've just yielded to the Holy Spirit on the direction that He is taking you, **"Yes Mode", God will begin to reveal to you what you will Birth.** Although, you're still clueless as to how you're going to get there exactly, you can begin to see clearer now, the direction you're headed.

Natural Pregnancy (2nd Trimester): Months 4-6 after conception **Spiritual Pregnancy (2nd Period):** Period of development and planning	• "Second trimester is typically an easier time — your first trimester worries are waning and morning sickness is finally letting up." • Changes in your mouth • Increased Appetite • As a result of increased blood circulation derived from the hormones, the body is gaining more nutrients. • Stretch Marks • Skin Discoloration • Belly begins to protrude. Others can notice the pregnancy • The expectant mother begins to feel movement • The proud family can discover the sex of their child through ultra-sound	• You're glad the stripping process is over. The good news is the 2nd period is not as rough as the 1st and 3rd period of spiritual pregnancy. • After you've said "Yes", you are eager to listen to the God (the Holy Spirit). (Note: it is understandable if you are in your 2nd or 3rd spiritual pregnancy to experience a rough transition as God requires you to leave behind what you felt was the ultimate Purpose for your life and now you're having to graduate to the next level, which may be very difficult for most. Sometimes, you must graduate a few levels before you reach your final destination.) Are you ready? • You're excited to gain understanding regarding your call so you long for God to speak to you on how to move forward. • You're excited about the vision, but you must slow down to hear the plan of the Lord. Take one day at a time. Remain in God's presence and seek Him early so that you may properly proceed daily. • *Note:* He will not tell you everything at once. Otherwise you could become overwhelmed and He does not want that.

PERIOD OR PHASE	NATURAL PREGNANCY	SPIRITUAL PREGNANCY
Natural Pregnancy (2nd Trimester): Months 4-6 after conception **Spiritual Pregnancy (2nd Period):** Period of development and planning - *continued*	• There has been major development in the child by the end of the 2nd trimester and babies have been known to live outside of the mother's womb by this time.	• You may feel that you know how you should proceed with the vision. Be sure to listen for which course He wants you to take, (Traditional Education or Supernatural Certification – Certified by the Holy Spirit or both) • An Increase in the level of confidence and joy you have regarding this pregnancy and God's plan for you concerning this spiritual pregnancy. • You're not the only one that knows of your pregnancy because you're starting to talk about the changes and people can just see the transition in your life (your attitude, your lifestyle….) • You're starting to get excited about the birth because you're seeing things come together. • You may experience many Braxton Hicks Contractions as expectant mother's experience in the natural during the 3rd trimester – prepping you for the delivery. You will feel that you are going to deliver this Purpose any day now; but there's yet a little while to go before your delivery comes.

• You will be challenged from the enemy. You must stand on guard for the spirit of distraction in this period via (work, circumstances beyond your control, family and friends, your own desires, activities, etc.); as well as laziness (rise when God tells you to rise and go when God says to go!).

• Your faith will increase and you will definitely trust God more than you've ever trusted Him in the past.

• You will get a closer walk with God as a result of your constant communication with Him. How EXCITING!

• As you transition to the third period of your pregnancy, you have been before the Lord for a while as He has given you the plan, you've made new encounters, you're now preparing in the physical, things around you as God prepares you for *Labor* and *Delivery* process.

PERIOD OR PHASE	NATURAL PREGNANCY	SPIRITUAL PREGNANCY
Natural Pregnancy: 3rd **Trimester:** Months 7-9 after conception **Spiritual Pregnancy: 3rd** **Period:** Period of Delivery - Planning and Development	• The baby begins to settle in position for birth, but can cause some discomfort to the expectant mother. • Varicose Veins caused by the extra volume of blood produced during pregnancy which is essential to support two growing bodies. • Shortness of breath caused by the repositioning of the internal organs. • Braxton Hicks Contractions which is when uterus is tightening up as it gearing the body for the big day. However, these are irregular Contractions. • Many expectant women suffer insomnia and can be a result of anxiety of the birth	• How long is delivery? Truly, only God knows! But stand guarded and get in position for the Great Victory! • You may feel anxiety because "you" are ready to deliver now! • As your spiritual contractions increase, you will definitely need to praise and worship God (giving thanks for the manifestation of His promise to you) and invite joy into your life daily for strength – keep your eye on the Almighty God so that you can stay the course • You may feel a lack of confidence, doubt, fear, and unbelief magnified. Let's not mention the distractions and the seducing spirits that may present itself as a light in this period! Got Armor? • The closer you near the laboring process, you will get more excited than you ever have in spite of the spiritual battle that you may be facing. You can see clearer now.

- Often, the expectant mother experiences changes in their eyesight – it seems to be less sharp

- Frequently the body begins to release fluid due to the position of the baby on the uterus

- Expectant mother's begin to walk differently due to the growth of the baby

- The true contractions will begin just prior to delivery – labor process will then begin – the contractions start out further apart and then get progressively closer together. Remember: Just as no two pregnancies are the same, no two labors are the same.

- Regardless of what challenges the expectant mother may have experienced during her pregnancy, she generally has faith that her baby will be fine. Therefore, she begins to prepare for the baby to come home (preparing the room, baby shower).

- You may actually feel like you just want to jump on the other side – you visualize yourself constantly in the manifestation of God's promise to you.

- You will begin to feel like there is nothing else for you to do but birth the gift. You are awaiting delivery and feel that you have prepared all you can. "What else could possibly need to be done?"

PERIOD OR PHASE	NATURAL PREGNANCY	SPIRITUAL PREGNANCY
Natural Labor/ Manifestation: Push out that baby! **4th Period - Spiritual Labor/Manifestation:** PRAISE into your True Purpose - Your life of fulfillment!	• The expectant mother will experience pain in this process, but the birth of her gift will make up for everything! • Phase I (Early (Latent) Labor): The cervix begins to dilate and the expectant mother will experience mild to moderate contractions. • Phase II (Active Labor): The contractions will grow stronger and longer during active labor. By this time the expectant mother is in the hospital or birthing place. • Phase III (Transitional (Advanced) Labor: "The last most intensive and fortunately shortest stage – but the contractions are very strong at this point."	• This is the toughest period in your Spiritual Pregnancy! • Phase I (Early Spiritual [Latent] Labor: Spiritual Braxton Hick will increase (combined feelings of overwhelmed [e.g. feeling slightly off task] and excited. You are ready to manifest right now but you must stay the course because it's not time! • Phase II (Active Spiritual Labor): You will really experience obstacle in this period! You thought your faith was challenged in Delivery, you haven't seen anything, but stay the course. You're almost there! Remember: The enemy is not happy that you're getting ready to manifest the promise. • Phase III (Spiritual Transitional Labor): You are actively getting into position. However, you may not know if you should Praise or Cry. It's oK, turn up your Praise (your highest thanks and recognition of your belief) and stand NO MATTER what comes your way!

The Manifestation…	• "You're almost at the finish line (or more accurately, the baby is). But getting there is going to take a little pushing — literally." • The baby is born!	• PRAISE! PRAISE! PRAISE! PRAISE! • Glory to God! Another Spiritual Birth has taken place! Oh my Lord! Are there twins, or do we see quintets…? Just praise God and enjoy this one for now unless God tells you to continue towards the next pregnancy, while maintaining this one (it's likely).
After Birth	• The placenta is released from the expectant mother's womb.	• This is the time to give Praise and Glory to God for a successful delivery and seek wisdom on how to maintain what He has blessed you with via ministry, home, lifestyle…
Postpartum Depression (Natural/Spiritual)	• "More severe than the more common baby blues, postpartum depression is characterized by crying, irritability, sleep problems, restlessness, feelings of hopelessness, and the inability to care for the baby. Many women suffering from postpartum depression need professional treatment."	• To put aside what God has given you, usually as a result of feelings of unworthiness, your perception of what was delivered (maybe you've noticed flaws in the work and want to hold on to it), feelings of doubt and fear of failing at what God has Purposed in your life, you hold back. Thereby, holding up someone's salvation. "As you carried God's Purpose, you will maintain God's Purpose – through "His" Guidance and Power!" Therefore, release what God has given to you in the confidence that what has been done through was God's power, anointing, and divine order for your life!

PERIOD OR PHASE	NATURAL PREGNANCY	SPIRITUAL PREGNANCY
Abortion (Natural/Spiritual)	• When a pregnancy is deliberately terminated.	• When you purposely avoid the call or choose not to move forward with God's plan for your life your True Purpose. Most times as a result of where you feel that you are currently in God, for the lack of money to move forward, or you just simply refuse to yield because "you're" not ready!
Premature Birth	• To deliver the baby prior to term, which is 37 weeks.	• The process of delivering prior to God's timing – you've moved ahead of God in His plan.
Pregnancy Duration	• Full term pregnancy is 9 months (42 weeks)	• Based on current observation, about 1 year from the 1st Period. This time varies from pregnancy to pregnancy and person to person.

Many are not aware of the term "Spiritual Pregnancy" (the process of birthing True Purpose into your life - a life of TOTAL fulfillment); however, many have successfully birthed "God's Plan – their True Purpose" in their lives without this revelation, Glory to God! To bring an understanding to such an intangible, blind, and for many, scary yet fulfilling process to all, is revolutionary and will result in more spiritual births (more people attaining their True Purpose - a life of TOTAL FULFILLMENT!) upon the earth. Thereby, making a more peaceful, joyful, confident, free, and fulfilled people all over the earth!

APPENDIX III

SCRIPTURES TO REFERENCE DURING YOUR SPIRITUAL PREGNANCY

God planned for the maturity of the times

Ephesians 1:10

[He planned] for the maturity of the times and the climax of the ages to unify all things and head them up and consummate them in Christ, [both] things in heaven and things on the earth.

God has already planned your life!

Ephesians 2:10

For we are God's [own] handiwork (His workmanship), recreated in Christ Jesus, [born new] that we may do those good works which God predestined (planned beforehand) for us [taking paths which He prepared ahead of time], that we should walk in them [living the good life which He prearranged and made ready for us to live].

Jesus was instructed by the Holy Spirit

Acts 10:38

How God anointed and consecrated Jesus of Nazareth with the [Holy] Spirit and with strength and ability and power; how He went about doing good and, in particular, curing all who were harassed and oppressed by [the power of] the devil, for God was with Him.

Jesus was formed here in the flesh

I Peter 2:21

For even to this were you called [it is inseparable from your vocation]. For Christ also suffered for you, leaving you [His personal] example, so that you should follow in His footsteps.

Jesus was led by the Holy Spirit

Luke 2:27

And prompted by the [Holy] Spirit, he came into the temple [enclosure]; and when the parents brought in the little child Jesus to do for Him what was customary according to the Law.

Luke 4:1

Then Jesus, full of and controlled by the Holy Spirit, returned from the Jordan and was led in [by] the [Holy] Spirit

Jesus gives honor to God

Matthew 12:28

But if it is by the Spirit of God that I drive out the demons, then the kingdom of God has come upon you [before you expected it].

Be guided by the Holy Spirit

Romans 8:4

So that the righteous and just requirement of the Law might be fully met in us who live and move not in the ways of the flesh but in the ways of the Spirit [our lives governed not by the standards and according to the dictates of the flesh, but controlled by the Holy Spirit].

Romans 8:5

For those who are according to the flesh and are controlled by its unholy desires set their minds on and [Joseph Thayer, A Greek-English Lexicon.] pursue those things which gratify the flesh, but those who are according to the Spirit and are controlled by the desires of the Spirit set their minds on and [Joseph Thayer, A Greek-English Lexicon.] seek those things which gratify the [Holy] Spirit.

The Holy Spirit will teach you all things

John 14:26

But the Comforter (Counselor, Helper, Intercessor, Advocate, Strengthener, Standby), the Holy Spirit, Whom the Father will send in My name [in My place, to represent Me and act on My behalf], He will teach you all things. And He will cause you to recall (will remind you of, bring to your remembrance) everything I have told you.

A man controlled by the flesh, can not understand the things of the Holy Spirit

I Corinthians 2:14

But the natural, non-spiritual man does not accept or welcome or admit into his heart the gifts and teachings and revelations of the Spirit of God, for they are folly (meaningless nonsense) to him; and he is incapable of knowing them [of progressively recognizing, understanding, and becoming better acquainted with them] because they are spiritually discerned and estimated and appreciated.

To pray in the unknown tongue (pray in the Spirit) you edify and improve yourself

I Corinthians 14:4

He who speaks in a [strange] tongue edifies and improves himself, but he who prophesies [interpreting the divine will and purpose and teaching with inspiration] edifies and improves the church and promotes growth [in Christian wisdom, piety, holiness, and happiness].

Do not be conformed to this world

Romans 12:2

Do not be conformed to this world (this age), [fashioned after and adapted to its external, superficial customs], but be transformed (changed) by the [entire] renewal of your mind [by its new ideals and its new attitude], so that you may prove [for yourselves] what is the good and acceptable and perfect will of God, even the thing which is good and acceptable and perfect [in His sight for you].

Don't depend on your own understanding

Proverbs 3:5

Lean on, trust in, and be confident in the Lord with all your heart and mind and do not rely on your own insight or understanding.
No pain, no gain – To share in the glory, you must share in the suffering

Romans 8:17

And if we are [His] children, then we are [His] heirs also: heirs of God and fellow heirs with Christ [sharing His inheritance with Him]; only we must share His suffering if we are to share His glory.

No weapon formed against you shall prosper

Isaiah 54:17

But no weapon that is formed against you shall prosper, and every tongue that shall rise against you in judgment you shall show to be in the wrong. This [peace, righteousness, security, triumph over opposition] is the heritage of the servants of the Lord [those in whom the ideal Servant of the Lord is reproduced]; this is the righteousness or the vindication which they obtain from Me [this is that which I impart to them as their justification], says the Lord.

You are righteous through Jesus Christ!

Philippians 1:11

May you abound in and be filled with the fruits of righteousness (of right standing with God and right doing) which come through Jesus Christ (the Anointed One), to the honor and praise of God [that His glory may be both manifested and recognized].

Not by your own works but through the work of the crucifixion

II Corinthians 5:21

For our sake He made Christ [virtually] to be sin Who knew no sin, so that in and through Him we might become [endued with, viewed as being in, and examples of] the righteousness of God [what we ought to be, approved and acceptable and in right relationship with Him, by His goodness].

The power of the tongue

Proverbs 18:21

Death and life are in the power of the tongue, and they who indulge in it shall eat the fruit of it [for death or life].

Jesus was made in the likeness of sinful flesh

Romans 8:3

For God has done what the Law could not do, [its power] being weakened by the flesh [the entire nature of man without the Holy Spirit]. Sending His own Son in the guise of sinful flesh and as an offering for sin, [God] condemned sin in the flesh [subdued, overcame, deprived it of its power over all who accept that sacrifice],

Jesus admonishes us to deny our ways and to follow Him

Matthew 16:24

Then Jesus said to His disciples, If anyone desires to be My disciple, let him deny himself [disregard, lose sight of, and forget himself and his own interests] and take up his cross and follow Me [cleave steadfastly to Me, conform wholly to My example in living and, if need be, in dying, also].

As a result of the crucifixion, there is no condemnation

II Corinthians 5:21

For our sake He made Christ [virtually] to be sin Who knew no sin, so that in and through Him we might become [endued with, viewed as being in, and examples of] the righteousness of God [what we ought to be, approved and acceptable and in right relationship with Him, by His goodness].

Righteousness is through Jesus Christ

Romans 3:22 - 25

22Namely, the righteousness of God which comes by believing with personal trust and confident reliance on Jesus Christ (the Messiah). [And it is meant] for all who believe. For there is no distinction,

23Since all have sinned and are falling short of the honor and glory which God bestows and receives.

24[All] are justified and made upright and in right standing with God, freely and gratuitously by His grace (His unmerited favor and mercy), through the redemption which is [provided] in Christ Jesus,

25Whom God put forward [before the eyes of all] as a mercy seat and propitiation by His blood [the cleansing and life-giving sacrifice of atonement and reconciliation, to be received] through faith. This was to show God's righteousness, because in His divine forbearance He had passed over and ignored former sins without punishment.

God's word will not return unto you void

Isaiah 55:11

So shall My word be that goes forth out of My mouth: it shall not return to Me void [without producing any effect, useless], but it shall accomplish that which I please and purpose, and it shall prosper in the thing for which I sent it.

The joy of the Lord is your strength

Nehemiah 8:10

Then [Ezra] told them, Go your way, eat the fat, drink the sweet drink, and send portions to him for whom nothing is prepared; for this day is holy to our Lord. And be not grieved and depressed, for the joy of the Lord is your strength and stronghold.

God has given you love, power, and a sound mind

2 Timothy 1:7

For God did not give us a spirit of timidity (of cowardice, of craven and cringing and fawning fear), but [He has given us a spirit] of power and of love and of calm and well-balanced mind and discipline and self-control.

All things work together for the good

Romans 8:28

We are assured and know that [[Some manuscripts read, "God works all things with them."] God being a partner in their labor] all things work together and are [fitting into a plan] for good to and for those who love God and are called according to [His] design and purpose.

Don't let your freedom be an excuse to allow your flesh to control you

Galatians 5:16 - 18

16But I say, walk and live [habitually] in the [Holy] Spirit [responsive to and controlled and guided by the Spirit]; then you will certainly not gratify the cravings and desires of the flesh (of human nature without God).

17For the desires of the flesh are opposed to the [Holy] Spirit, and the [desires of the] Spirit are opposed to the flesh (godless human nature); for these are antagonistic to each other [continually withstanding and in conflict with each other], so that you are not free but are prevented from doing what you desire to do.

18But if you are guided (led) by the [Holy] Spirit, you are not subject to the Law.

How to become a child of God

Romans 10:8 - 10

8But what does it say? The Word (God's message in Christ) is near you, on your lips and in your heart; that is, the Word (the message, the basis and object) of faith which we preach,

9Because if you acknowledge and confess with your lips that Jesus is Lord and in your heart believe (adhere to, trust in, and rely on the truth) that God raised Him from the dead, you will be saved.

10For with the heart a person believes (adheres to, trusts in, and relies on Christ) and so is justified (declared righteous, acceptable to God), and with the mouth he confesses (declares openly and speaks out freely his faith) and confirms [his] salvation.

BIBLIOGRAPHY

1.   Walsch, Neale Donald. Conversations with God...an uncommon dialogue. First Hardcover Edition, Book 1. New York: G.P. Putnam's Sons, 1996

2.   Houghton Mifflin Company. The American Heritage College Dictionary, Third Edition. 1997, 1993

3.   Robeson, Jerry and Carol. Strongman's His Name...What's His Game? New Edition. Woodburn: Shiloh Publishing House, 1983

4.   Fornara, Stacy. Amplified Version, King James Version, 1995-2005 <http://www.bible.com>

5.   Nelson, Thomas, Inc. Extreme Teem Bible. The Holy Bible New Century Version. Fort Worth: World Bible Translation Center, 2001.

6.   Thomas Nelson, Inc., Extreme Teen Bible. The Holy Bible, New Century Version. Fort Worth. 2001

7.   Goldman, Jonathan L. Webster's New World, Pocket Dictionary. Fourth Edition. Wiley Publishing, Inc. Cleveland: 2000

8.   Etheridge, Eric. "The Freedom Riders". The Oprah Magazine. May 2008, pgs. 316-322 (321).

9.   American Press. "Thousands attend Parks' funeral – Race and ethnicity." MSNBC. http://msnbc.msn.com/id/9893832/ (2/ Nov/2005).

10.   The Estate of Martin Luther King, Jr. "The Autobiography of Martin Luther King, Jr." Chapter 16: The Albany Movement. http://www.standford.edu/group/King/publications/autobiography/chp_16.htm (Diary: 30/Jan/1961, 21/May/1961, 15/Dec/1961, 16/Dec/1961, 10/July/1962, 12/July/1962, 22/July/1962, 26/July/1962, 10/Aug/1962)

AUTHOR BIOGRAPHY

Studio: GMD Studios, Brighton, Michigan
Hair by: Tish Hogan; Ferndale, Michigan

Currently, Princess-O'dilia is an Entrepreneur, Author, Writer, Poet, Singer, Song-writer, Motivational Inspirational Speaker, Educator and Radio Talk Show Host.

Princess-O'dilia as an overcome victim of physical, emotional, mental, and verbal abuse endured for years, and an Entrepreneur for over a decade, now with transparency and years of personal experience of spiritual pregnancy, shares with conviction, compassion, wit and passion the reality of God's equipping power within us all, to help us discover and manifest the life of TOTAL fulfillment that we all seek!

As the Author of **THE ARMOR OF GOD** (2B-Real Publishing) and the **PURPOSE PLANNER**, Princess-Odilia continues to be profoundly inspired as she now receives insight of the intangible keys that every man and woman need to accomplish the journey to their Destiny in her new book, **PREGNANT IN THE SPIRIT**.

274

Princess-O'dilia dives deep beyond the superficial layers of fear and complacency to unearth the hidden potential within each of us.

As an inspired authority on destiny fulfillment, her insight gives a practical road map with fresh perspective.

She delivers practical keys for those in search of answers. Whether in turmoil or transition, her deep well of divine inspiration brings clarity and insight of the intangible and inevitable road to destiny and a clear path to finish the course to achieve lasting peace, true happiness, spiritual freedom, joy, and confidence of your life's direction and its outcome.

As a respected inspirational Author and Speaker, she has paved the way to fulfillment in ministry and entrepreneurship. Princess-O'dilia's motivational speaking and books, share with conviction, compassion and transparent honesty, her painful journey to overcome abuse, depression, financial hardship and heartache to live her dreams and achieve success. She shares and enlightens of God's equipping power within us, giving us the keys to birthing a profound life of TOTAL fulfillment that would not otherwise be attainable.

As a prolific writer, poet and highly sought after Consultant and Speaker, Princess-O'dilia's outreach has reached to the coast of Africa, Asia and Russia. Her mission is to spread the message of freedom and love without condemnation, but justification through the sacrifice of Jesus Christ and the love of God.

As an inspiring Seminar Host and Educator, Princess-O'dilia is a respected Mentor in ministry and business. Often with standing room only crowds, she has instructed thousands at speaking engagements around the country.

Princess-O'dilia is the CEO and Founder since 2001 of the non-profit corporation Bountiful Opportunities Group, Inc., Former CEO and Co-Founder of Opportunity First Financial Services, LLC and she is the founder of Bountiful Group Financial Services, LLC, a successful Real Estate Investment and Consulting Firm. She also founded a Real Estate Continuing Educational Center in the Metropolitan Detroit Area derived from the Continuing Adult Ed Real Estate Investment Courses she founded and taught at Marygrove College in Detroit, MI from 2000-2003.

Princess-O'dilia has expanded Bountiful Opportunities Group, Inc. (A.D.B.A. BG Ministries), and its mission of helping others help themselves through educational and outreach services by spreading the message of TOTAL fulfillment achievement, via conducting Spiritual Birthing (Coaching) Seminars and Workshops, Purpose Planning Workshops, Spiritual Warfare Workshops, Individual Consultations, and itinerate Speaking Engagements in Churches, Community Venues, and Shelters on Spiritual Birthing, Life Coaching, and Abuse.

Her radio talk show Quiet No More! is heard weekly on Blog Talk Radio, Thursdays at 12:00 p.m.

Princess-O'dilia has personally consulted and educated thousands in Real Estate Investment as well as helped 1000s of families in jeopardy of foreclosure through her seminars and acclaimed Radio Talk shows: "The Moment of Hope" (Radio One-Detroit and Indianapolis) and "Keepin' It Real" (Radio One-Detroit, MI) .

As a singer and songwriter, Princess-O'dilia's God-inspired music has been highly acclaimed by Arista Records and other noted producers and artists in the industry.

She is a single mother of two beautiful children.

WHY DID SHE CHANGE HER NAME?

PRINCESS-O`DILIA (No last name)…
FKA: Lisa R. Blanding

"Since a child I had a desire to change my name. As an adult, the desire became stronger. I initially hesitated because I didn't know what people would think of me, but after prayer and research, this name was chosen.

Many people have changed their names in the past. For example, Abram to Abraham (based on my experience, I can only imagine what he went through). Additionally, many musicians and stars have changed their name as well.

For me, at the age of 12 I knew that I had to change my name. From the age of 12 I had profound experiences that clued me of my destiny. At the age of 12, I began to build a personal relationship with God and began to ask questions, seeking purpose even then. At 12 I knew that there was a huge light at the end of the tunnel and knew that I would go through some things that I would overcome before I got there.

Although I was urged very strongly to change my name for years, it wasn't until I was in my 30s that I moved forward with the process. It was one day when I was "minding my own business" the urge came so strong that to ignore it I would not have been able to rest.

I searched as I allowed myself to be inspired to discover the chosen name within two days of me yielding to the strong urge. I initially rejected the concept even after the name was chosen and one day I received a definite sign that this was my destiny. I even questioned God if I should make it legal or make it just a stage name. Well, it was made apparent to me that it was to be legal so I completely yielded to this change.

It's interesting, I knew of no other Princess-O'dilia, nor did I like the name at first, but it was that strongest feeling, the urge that sort of forced my decision. After I had begun the process legally, I did further research and discovered that there was a Princess-Odilia (A.K.A. Lady-Odilia) before me. She was born blind and at the age of 12 a prophet was led by the Spirit to baptize her and he was told that she would see when she came up from the water. This came to pass and she was able to see from that moment. She suffered tremendously in her time (B.C.) because of this miracle, but persevered. She later started schools for the blind and she was an intercessor. She impacted lives all over the world (particularly in the Catholic community).

Just prior to me changing my name, my life had gone in a completely different direction. I was doing things I never thought I would. I was teaching, counseling, consulting, and had begun interceding for many people. I never imagined that. It's very interesting how my life's purpose is almost parallel to what her life's purpose and mission was - Helping people by teaching and interceding for others.

My name is most humbling and I am honored to have been given this name."

Princess-O'dilia

Princess: I'm a child of the King (Our Father God in Heaven, the Creator)
O'dilia: Praise God, wealthy, rich girl
Association: Hebrew and German

New Release October 2009!

Princess-O`dilia will get naked before the world with her autobiography of a life of abuse, To Whom It May Concern: Through Raw Eyes – An Autobiography of Abuse. Princess-O`dilia and her two triumphant children speak out about their traumatic life of abuse and the spiritual infections of weakness and fear that plagued the life of Princess-O'dilia and influenced her choices for years. As Princess-Odilia speaks out about her life, she receives the interpretation through the raw eyes of her children of how they viewed her and how her choices impacted their lives. It's quite interesting to learn how they all triumphed once Princess-O'dilia got a clue of what was really going on with her!

"It's interesting to hear how a child views the experience of abuse. Children see everything through raw-innocent eyes, where as we see things optimistically.

What I've learned about the impact of my choices hurt, but this story has not only helped heal our wounds but it will help an infinite number of families and lives as we keep it real about our lives. For our naked truth, many will be clothed with hope, life, freedom, happiness and deliverance from abuse – which is a major key to a life of TOTAL fulfillment."

Princess-O'dilia

Resource Page

KNOWING IS HALF THE BATTLE!

Today, the economy is unstable. Who or What can you trust? People are lacking confidence about their future all over the world.

Share Pregnant in the Spirit, a priceless gift, with someone that you know is seeking direction, experiencing turmoil, transition, or is not TOTALLY fulfilled!

- Clarity
- Understanding
- Confidence and Peace

IT'S PRICELESS!

NOTE: PREGNANT IN THE SPIRIT STUDY GUIDE WILL BE AVAILABLE FOR PURCHASE IN MARCH 2009 – ORDER TODAY!

Princess-Odilia is available for speaking, teaching, and interviews. For more information, please contact Terrie Price at (888) 982-4377 or email your request to t.price@brealpublishing.com. Mail all correspondences to: 1000 S. Old Woodward, Ste. 105-2; Birmingham, MI 48009 or Fax: (248) 247-1199. Visit Princess-O`dilia on-line today at www.princessodilia.com.

ORDERING INSTRUCTIONS

1)   You may order on-line at: www.brealpublishing.com, www.amazon.com, www.borders.com and www.barnesandnoble. com, www.stl-distribution.com

2)   You may also order by mailing the attached completed form below:

Payment Options	✓	Payment Options	✓
Check		Visa	
Money Order		Master Card	
Credit Card #			
Expiration Date			
Printed Name			
Address			
City, State, Zip Code			
Signature			

Additional Cost for Normal Shipping: $4.00

Additional Costs for Special Shipping:
Next Day: $14.00
2-3 Day: $8.00

Make checks payable or money orders payable to
2B~Real Publishing, LLC.

ORDER FORM

Item	Qty	Description	Total
PISBK		Pregnant in the Spirit (19.95 each)	
PISSG		Pregnant in the Spirit – Study Guide (15.95 each)	
PRP		Jehovah – Your Provider Poster (5.95 each)	
TWCBK		To Whom it May Concern (15.95-Pre Order)	
AOGBK		The Armor of God (15.95 each)	
		SUBTOTAL	
		Shipping and Handling	
		TOTAL	

Mail ordering form to: 2B~Real Publishing;

1000 S. Old Woodward, Suite 105-2; Birmingham, MI 48009.

Please visit www.brealpublishing.com for more products and

special offerings.

CPSIA information can be obtained
at www.ICGtesting.com
Printed in the USA
FFHW020808290519
52708222-58213FF